SIMPLE GIVING

SIMPLE GIVING

Easy Ways to Give Every Day

Jennifer Iacovelli

JEREMY P. TARCHER/PENGUIN
an imprint of Penguin Random House
New York

JEREMY P. TARCHER/PENGUIN
An imprint of Penguin Random House LLC
375 Hudson Street
New York, New York 10014

Most Tarcher/Penguin books are available at special quantity discounts for
bulk purchase for sales promotions, premiums, fund-raising, and educational
needs. Special books or book excerpts also can be created to fit specific
needs. For details, write: SpecialMarkets@penguinrandomhouse.com.

Library of Congress Cataloging-in-Publication Data

Iacovelli, Jennifer.
Simple giving : easy ways to give every day / Jennifer Iacovelli.
pages cm
Summary: "Most people think they have to donate a lot of time and money in order
to make a difference. But there are simple ways to integrate giving into our personal
and professional lives that don't involve either. In Simple Giving, Jennifer Iacovelli
shows us how to make giving a part of our daily routines"—Provided by publisher.
ISBN 978-0-399-17245-8 (paperback)
1. Self-actualization (Psychology)   2. Generosity.
3. Nonprofit organizations.   I. Title.
BF637.S4.I23 2015
177'.7—dc23
2015022157

Printed in the United States of America
1   3   5   7   9   10   8   6   4   2

Book design by Lauren Kolm

To my boys, Gavin and Biz, my most inspiring simple givers.
I love you a gazillion a million beyond thirty.

CONTENTS

ACKNOWLEDGMENTS

From concept to completion, this book has proved to be an incredible journey for me. A journey—much like my giving journey—filled with life lessons and soul-shining moments.

While this is by no means an exhaustive list, there are a few people I'd like to publicly thank for helping me in this journey:

First and foremost, my literary agent and (former) father-in-law, Bruce Barbour, whose support, encouragement, knowledge, and love mean the world to me.

Ilene Evans and Alexa Bigwarfe, who from the very beginning helped keep me accountable and inspired me to write. Thank you also to Alexa for those weekly phone calls and help with research.

Dr. Greg Evans, who shared with me his knowledge of

positive psychology and helped me with resources for this book.

My parents, who took the boys when I desperately needed to write.

Joanna Ng, my editor, and everyone at Tarcher/Penguin who have made this process much less overwhelming for me.

All of the regular readers of my blog, Another Jennifer, who have given me so much love and encouragement over the years and embraced my writing on philanthropy from the very beginning.

Every person I have interviewed for this book and for my Philanthropy Friday series. Every one of you inspires me beyond words. Thank you for taking the time to share your passions with me so that I can share them with the world.

1 Acting on the Pull to Give

*Give what you have. To someone, it may be
better than you dare to think.*

Henry Wadsworth Longfellow

I admit it. I am an idealist and want to change the world. I want to leave it in a better place than when I first visited it. I want to donate my time, money, and voice to right the wrongs of the world. I want my kids to be solid citizens who give without hesitation because it's the right thing to do.

In theory, who doesn't, right?

Yet many people think that only rich people can make a real difference. They question how a small donation can make any impact at all. Or maybe they just don't know where to start when it comes to giving back. My experience in the non-profit world has shown me that a small contribution can make a big difference in someone's life. And it doesn't always have to involve money or volunteer time. Sometimes, a simple gesture or voice of support is all that's needed.

I've worked in the behavioral health field since 2004 and in addiction treatment since 2006. Specifically, my job has been to communicate the good work that organizations do to help people overcome substance abuse and mental health struggles in order to live better lives. It's a tough sell, because society doesn't always regard people with addiction and mental health problems highly. There is stigma attached, particularly with women. Not everyone wants to support a homeless, heroin-addicted woman who is pregnant and neglecting her toddler or a wealthy lawyer who drank away her practice and her family.

A women in her most desperate moment—sometimes in an orange prison suit and shackles—walking through the doors of a treatment center is the most courageous thing I have witnessed in my career, to the point where I question whether I would have the courage to do the same.

One of the most valuable gifts you can give is the gift of support. I know this because I have seen the faces of women when they walk through those doors—unsure of the road ahead of them but desperate to get off the one they are on—completely change due to the smile from the person at the front desk. They might be flanked by prison guards or looking like they haven't slept or showered in days. Some might even still be drunk or high. But that first person smiling at you and welcoming you without judgment, despite all that you've done wrong prior to coming to that building, creates a changing point in your life.

My point with this story—and with this book—is that giving is more than just donating money or volunteering time. There are so many simple ways you can give back every day.

MY PULL TO GIVE

When I first started my blog, Another Jennifer, in February 2010, I was yearning for a creative outlet. I had been working in public communications in the nonprofit sector for about six years, and I was getting burnt out. The work was rewarding, but I found myself frustrated with my perceived lack of progress. I felt like I was always asking people for money to support our work or urging legislators not to cut funding or explaining the importance of treatment in general. And I was.

I found myself questioning why people didn't care more. Why didn't they understand that there were people out there who needed help? Of course, if you work in the nonprofit sector, you are constantly reminded of the need that is out there. When you are not aware of a problem in your community, then caring or helping is not on the priority list. Helping is simply not on the radar.

Frustrated, I started to explore the topic of philanthropy—among other things—on my blog. I started with the meaning of philanthropy. In one of my first giving-related blog posts, I wrote,

> "One of my goals for 2011 is to live more philanthropically (and figure out what this means in the process)." I even made it part of my new motto/slogan.
>
> My thought is that I am at the point in my life when I have the resources to give back in a more meaningful way. But what does it mean to give back? And how do I build philanthropy into my everyday life? (Just working for a non-profit doesn't count.)[1]

I knew I wanted to do more in terms of giving, but I didn't know how to approach the task. In this post, I reviewed a few formal definitions of *philanthropy*. I came to the conclusion that a common theme among the definitions was the act of supporting or bettering humankind. Donating money was not the key factor in defining philanthropy. This was an eye-opening discovery for me, as it made me think differently about the concept of giving back.

Not long after I wrote this post and started to explore how I could give back in a more meaningful way, I came across a blog post by Matthew Smith entitled "The Difference Between Charity and Philanthropy."[2] He noted that the difference between these two words "makes the biggest impact on the world around us." A lightbulb went off in my head when I read one specific sentence in this simple post: "Charity is giving . . . philanthropy is doing."

The word *charity* tends to have a negative connotation associated with it, much like the word *addiction*. We tend to give to charity because we feel like we have to, because there's an immediate need, not because we really want to. The example of the devastating Haiti earthquake comes to mind— when $1.3 billion was raised by U.S. relief groups alone in the six months following the event.[3] We often give and move on to the next thing that's happening in our life. There is not much follow-up involved.

To use Matthew's words:

Whereas charity is essential to address immediate needs, philanthropy is the means by which individuals and nonprofit agencies achieve their greater missions. Philanthropy is breaking down the stereotype that an ex-offender can't contribute to a business and society at-large. Philanthropy is building a well for a remote village in East Africa. Philanthropy is changing hearts and minds and cultures, it's righting wrongs, it's making the world a better place.

While philanthropy is surely more challenging than charity because it involves a long-term commitment, it is also much more rewarding.

Part of the problem people have with philanthropy is that they don't know how to give. This might seem odd, but sometimes a person's good intentions actually create more work for than actually help a nonprofit.

On the development side of the nonprofit world, I was often in charge of accepting in-kind donations of goods or services. More specifically, saying "no" to donations. I became the point person because I could explain to people that though we appreciated their kindness, their gifts just weren't needed.

Some people would actually get angry with me when I rejected their gifts. I would carefully note that, as a nonprofit, we didn't have the storage to keep items we couldn't use immediately. Donations like bags full of used clothing and baby furniture weren't accepted due to health and safety reasons. Even if they were clean and fairly new, we had to consider the fact that these items were being introduced to an inpatient facility that had a steady flow of clients and staff constantly going through its doors. There was no guarantee that we'd have clients who would fit into the clothing or that the baby gear had not been recalled in the past. It was more efficient for the agency to work with other nonprofits in the community to provide these items.

Sensing the deflated ego of the eager donor, I would instead offer guidance as to where their gift might have a more beneficial impact. I would also share the agency's current wish list or note that a monetary donation would often give us the opportunity to provide for a client's needs faster than an in-kind donation since day-to-day needs changed so quickly. If the person revealed that they were in recovery, I might encourage them to share their success story with our clients, a process that often has a lasting, positive impact on a person's recovery. This strategy proved successful because now the potential donor knew exactly how to make the most impact with their gift. They were often thankful for this interaction and left feeling empowered.

These interactions with would-be donors also inspired me. Though I didn't realize it at the time, these exchanges taught me that with a little direction and education, anyone could improve her philanthropic impact.

HOW I BEGAN TO GIVE

As my blog and my definition of giving developed, I decided to start a Philanthropy Friday series. The idea was to share the stories of people and businesses that incorporated philanthropy into their everyday routines. Honestly, I was looking for ideas for my own personal life and business. What better way to find new ways to give than to explore the unique ways in which people were already giving? The stories were out there, and I was on a mission to find them.

My first post was about simple ways to give that didn't involve money.[4] The prompt came from the Talk About Giving blog, where each week a question is asked about giving.[5] The purpose is to encourage readers to have conversations about the questions with family members, particularly kids. That week, the question was, "Can we give something other than money?"

In that first post, I wrote about how a colleague of my then husband's was going through a tough time because his three-year-old daughter was fighting cancer. She and her older sister were roughly the same age as our boys, and I couldn't fathom how hard it must be to see your own child suffer. We talked with our kids about how the family was a lot like us, and how they could use some love and support to help them get through the cancer treatment. We talked about how the treatment would make the girl sick and lose her hair. We talked about how it might not even help her get better.

My older son asked what we could do to help the little girl. Ultimately, we decided that what she really needed was some smiles and support. My son, who was six at the time, drew a beautiful picture filled with bright colors. We found out later that she loved getting pictures and letters from people she didn't know, which encouraged my son to send even more. His contribution made a difference in someone's life when she really needed it. The pictures made the little girl feel good and made my son feel like he was helping her get better.

After that first article, I started to post inquiries to find people and businesses that I could feature in my new series. I wanted to find everyday people and small businesses, not just the big names that everyone hears. Since I started the series in October of 2011, I've featured more than 150 stories of giving. Not only did I find great people to feature but they were also eager to talk to me about their philanthropic endeavors and to inspire others to apply the same giving practices. They truly wanted to share their stories, many of which you will read about in this book.

By the end of 2011, I decided to start my own giving pledge. I didn't feel like I was donating enough of my own money to charity. Though we certainly were not rich, we knew that we could afford to give more. When we looked at our charitable donations for the year at tax time, we were disappointed in ourselves.

We found ourselves asking questions like, how can we give more? How can we make donating a percentage of our earnings to charity a habit and not an afterthought? Like most people, donating money was not on our minds on a regular basis, even if I did work for a nonprofit agency. December tends to be the most popular time to give simply because it's the holiday giving season, and people are thinking about tax deductions. How could we give year-round?

My giving pledge was simple. I pledged to donate money to at least one nonprofit each month. I made my pledge public on my blog, and I wrote about the causes I donated to each month and why I chose to give to those causes. Writing about my donations was a way for me to keep the act of giving in the forefront of my life while also keeping me accountable for my pledge. My posts also serve as inspiration to my readers.

The pledge made me think more about where and why I gave. It also opened up more conversations about giving in our household. I found myself giving for very personal reasons, because a cause affected me directly. I also found myself donating money to support friends or colleagues. Sometimes, as in the case of Hurricane Sandy or the shooting at Sandy Hook Elementary School, I gave because I felt like I needed to. The more I gave, the more opportunities to give seemed to present themselves.

After taking on these philanthropic endeavors via my blog, I was invited to join the Global Team of 200, a group of women bloggers who focus on raising awareness for the causes of maternal health, children, hunger, and women and girls. This group allows me to use my voice and my blog to advocate and support the work of nonprofit organizations all over the globe. It has also connected me to like-minded bloggers, mothers and socially conscious women. I was honored to represent the team and Mom Bloggers for Social Good during an insight trip to Nicaragua with WaterAid America during World Water Day in 2014.

As you can see, while I did incorporate donating money into my everyday life, not all of my endeavors involved cash. As I further explored the ways in which people and businesses gave back, I observed several other models that can be just as effective. In particular, I've noted six specific giving models that all givers can incorporate in their lives right now, whether you are a stay-at-home mom, a budding blogger, or an entrepreneur. These six models are everyday acts of kindness, traditional philanthropy, shopping with a conscience, taking action

on your passion, giving as a business model, and giving it forward (or modeling giving to inspire others to act).

A BROADER DEFINITION OF GIVING

Before going any further, let me be clear about what I mean by
giving. As you can tell by now, my definitions of *giving* and
philanthropy are broader than their traditional meanings.

When I Googled "giving definition," I found the following:

GIVING   *present participle of give (Verb)*

> *Freely transfer the possession of (something) to
> (someone); hand over to: "they gave her water."*

> *Bestow (love, affection, or other emotional support):
> "his parents gave him encouragement"; "he was very
> giving and supportive."*

When I looked up "philanthropy definition" in Google, I
found this definition:

PHILANTHROPY   *(Noun)*

> *The desire to promote the welfare of others, expressed
> esp. by the generous donation of money to good causes.*

A philanthropic institution; a charity.

Synonyms
charity—benevolence—beneficence

I should note that you could look up these and other giving-related terms in a number of sources and come up with several definitions. I also suspect that if you asked ten people to define these terms, you would receive ten different answers. I believe the reason for this discrepancy is the personal nature of giving.

I'd like to propose a definition of giving that incorporates a bit of both of the above explanations of giving and philanthropy because I think giving should involve both the act of helping a cause and the emotional drive that inspires the act.

Whether we give back through volunteering at a soup kitchen or donating money, we do so for our own personal reasons. We might not realize it, but we often give because it makes us feel good as well. A mom might offer her time to a schoolteacher because she knows it will benefit her child. She also knows how much pressure the teacher is under to provide the best education possible for her students with limited resources. A president of a company may declare a day of service for his employees so that they can get some time away from the office.

He also knows that volunteering together may make his team stronger and give them a greater sense of purpose.

I noted that a common thread in my initial research on the definition of philanthropy had to do with "supporting or bettering humankind." If this were true, then would advocating for an animal shelter not count as being philanthropic? There are, of course, many local and worldwide organizations dedicated to supporting animals, the environment, and natural resources. We need to be more specific about what we mean about giving.

To give back in a meaningful way, I believe you need two key components:

1. A person should genuinely want to make a positive impact.
2. The act should benefit someone or something else.

I use the word *act* because I think we need to think about more than just physical donations and volunteering. Throughout the book, I will illustrate these types of acts and how they benefit the giver and the receiver.

I also believe that we need to stop thinking that giving back is difficult or unattainable for some people. Just as the definitions differ, so do the ways in which we give. Everyone is different. We all have our own passions. Why should we all give in the same way?

If you stop and think about what is important to you and what kinds of giving make you feel the happiest, you can accomplish your own simple giving strategy.

Here are a just a few examples of simple giving:

- Calling your legislators about an issue important to you
- Shopping for gifts at a local store
- Writing about a largely unknown disease
- Holding a door open for a busy mom
- Picking up trash in your neighborhood
- Bringing doughnuts to the local fire department
- Checking up on an elderly neighbor
- Talking to your kids about giving back

Ideally, to be most effective in your philanthropic deeds over time, you also want to strive for two other key components:

1. The act should inspire others to do their own giving.
2. You want to make your giving sustainable over time.

These last two components, of course, are harder to achieve than the first two. This is where it becomes helpful to study successful giving models that have been applied by people just like you. It is also helpful to understand how giving improves our overall happiness and well-being.

THE BENEFITS OF GIVING

By now, I hope you are seeing the act of giving as more than donating money, goods, or time to a nonprofit organization or people less fortunate than yourself. Did you know that giving can also be good for your health?

Think about it. Have you ever had a complete stranger jump to your assistance when you were about to drop an armload of groceries as you attempted to open a door? Has a fellow parent given you that reassuring look just when you thought you were about to have a meltdown with your toddler in the middle of a store? Did someone let you go ahead of him as you were trying to take a difficult left-hand turn into traffic?

It feels good to be on the receiving end of a good deed, doesn't it? It might even inspire you to do a good deed for someone else. Paying it forward, if you will.

In a guest post on my blog, Dan Tomasulo, PhD, wrote "Theory, research and practice suggest it's wise to support any company that has generosity as a business model."[6] He cited research that showed when subjects were given money and told they could spend it on themselves or give it to others, they were happier being generous and giving it away. He observed that when a local farmer brings delicious fresh food that he's grown to tellers at his bank every week, they are appreciative and become the farmer's best form of advertising.

Children who perform random acts of kindness in school have also been found to be more accepting of their peers and thus more popular.[7] Researchers found that nine to eleven year olds who performed simple and intentional acts of kindness, like hugging their moms when they were stressed out or sharing their lunch, were kids whom their classmates wanted to spend more time with. At an age where bullying can become an issue, this finding can help kids not only become more accepting of other people but also encourage helping and generosity at a young age.

So why don't we practice these good deeds more often? Why don't we display generosity on a regular basis?

We live in a busy society where we often forget to stop and smell the roses. We rush to meetings or to drop off kids at school. We are parents, entrepreneurs, students, and employees. Sure, we care. But who has time to volunteer? And who knows where to start when it comes to giving?

The problem is that we sometimes forget to give. We get caught up in our busy lives and stop paying attention to those around us. Been there. Done that.

Imagine the impact we could make if we all did just one

simple good deed every day. Nothing big: just a simple good deed that might inspire others to "pay it forward" with another good deed. Imagine if we could come up with our own individual giving strategies to use in our personal and/or professional lives?

We're going to explore the psychology behind giving and new giving models in the next few chapters. And because everyone is different, you'll be offered several examples and resources to help you find the style of giving that fits you best, whether it's performing acts of kindness or developing a full-fledged social enterprise.

To help you in your giving exploration, each chapter will include the following:

- Examples and anecdotes of giving strategies that may be new to you
- Ideas and/or action steps you can execute now
- Resources to get you started

WHAT'S YOUR PULL?

I explained a bit about my pull to give. The truth is that I still feel like I need to give more. The more I give, the stronger the pull gets. That's how I know I'm working on the right giving model for my family and me. I am thinking about giving. I am giving. And I want to give more. As a blogger and a parent, I am inspiring others to give.

The exploration never ends because you and your giving habits are constantly evolving.

My questions to you: What's your pull to give? What compelled you to pick up this book? What moves you to want to give? What kind of legacy do you want to leave? Think about these questions as you read this book, pick out the giving tactics that work best for you, and craft your own giving model. The sky's the limit.

2　The Psychology of Giving

*I'm trying to broaden the scope of positive
psychology well beyond the smiley face.
Happiness is just one-fifth of what human
beings choose to do.*

Martin Seligman

Before we dive into the giving models, it's important to understand the psychology behind what makes us want to, and even need to, give. While it is easy to simply say that giving makes us feel good and it is the right thing to do, not all types of giving are created equally. Donating to the Red Cross after a natural disaster may make you content. But, chances are, that satisfaction will fade soon thereafter.

What kind of giving will make you feel like you are truly making a difference? Is it important for you to see the impact of your donation? Do you prefer to get your hands dirty and do some of the work yourself? Is your experience more meaningful when you share it with others? These are some questions to think about as you explore the different models of giving.

Happiness does not always come from the most obvious places. Understanding what drives you into action will help you figure out how to act on your pull to give and what kind of giving will be most meaningful to you.

HOW GIVING MAKES US HAPPY AND HEALTHY

There's an entire branch of psychology that focuses on happiness and what brings us meaning in life. Positive psychology is relatively new to the scientific world, but it has been gaining considerable momentum over the past few years. The basic difference between this new field of psychology and the traditional psychology model is that it focuses on how people can become more fulfilled in life. Traditionally, psychology has been more about dysfunction and diagnosing that dysfunction. As Martin Seligman noted in a past TED talk, psychologists had become "victimologists" and forgotten to develop interventions to make people happy in the first place.[1]

Martin Seligman is widely known as the father of positive psychology. He talks about the three paths to happiness—the pleasant life, the good life, and the meaningful life. The word *meaningful* is key. Giving and our own well-being are tied to meaningful actions and events. The meaningful life is where we find the most happiness.

Several studies have shown that people are happier spending money on others than on themselves.[2] Compared to those who were told to spend money on themselves, the participants who were involved in "prosocial spending," or spending money on others, reported being happier. The amount of money did not make a difference either. Similar results were found when people were given $5 and $20.

I remember the first time I took my oldest son to shop for a child in need. It was during the holiday season, and we had a wish list from a local boy about the same age as my son. At first, my son thought it was funny that things like toothpaste and soap were included along with books and a toy truck. I explained that not everyone was as fortunate as we were to be able to afford basic toiletry items. I gave him a budget and walked with him around the store to pick out our gifts. While he wanted to fulfill every single item on the list, he quickly learned to pick and choose which items would be most important and impactful for the boy. He chose some of the basic necessities and two toys, ensuring the boy would have what he needed as well as some fun things to play with. He was satisfied with his decision because he would have used the items himself.

A Gallup World Poll survey between 2006 and 2008 found that those who donated to charity in the past month had higher life satisfaction, whether they lived in a rich or a poor country. Even children as young as two years old have been found to be happier when they give treats to others versus being given treats.

While it makes sense that the act of giving feels good, the most meaningful giving seems to come when the experience is shared with another person. For example, one study handed out $10 Starbucks gift cards in four different ways.[3] Some participants were instructed to give the card away to someone else, while others were told to take someone out for coffee. Some recipients were to get coffee alone and spend the gift card on themselves, while others could bring a friend, but only spend the gift card on themselves. When participants were asked to describe their experience and report their level of happiness at the end of the day, those that spent the gift card money on someone else while also spending time with that person were the happiest. Those participants were not only benefiting from the act of giving but they were also more active participants in the giving experience.

Similar results have been found in a work setting.[4] Employees who were given a bonus to spend on charity showed higher job satisfaction and happiness than those who received no bonus at all. In another study, employees were given money to spend on either themselves or their teammates at work. As in the previously mentioned studies, the givers showed the most positive results. Contrary to what some bosses and employees might believe, these studies also show that while bonuses make employees happy for a period of time, they do not necessarily ensure happiness or job satisfaction in the long run.

When you consider the findings of these studies, it's no wonder that my son felt more satisfied when he was given the opportunity to spend money on someone else and could share the experience with me. He knew he was helping to give a boy a brighter holiday by providing him with specific items he needed. Thoughtfully handpicking those items with me—and thus playing an active part in the giving experience—was a lot more meaningful than simply grabbing a toy and throwing it in a donation bin right before Christmas.

Who doesn't want to lead a happier life, right? Not only does giving appear to be a key component to happiness, but it also has positive effects on our physical health.

A study by Steve Cole and Barbara Frederickson actually found lower inflammation levels in people who lived a life full of purpose and meaning. Inflammation, which reaches high levels in those who live with stress and is linked to cancer and other diseases, often occurred in those who lived the "good life."[5] It was those whose lives included compassion, altruism, and greater meaning that had lower levels.

A study published in the *Journal of Research in Personality* illustrated that a meaningful life that includes acknowledging gifts received from others helps create a sense of belonging.[6] A combination of grit—defined as "the long-term interests and passions, and willingness to persevere through obstacles and setbacks to make progress toward goals aligned or separate from these passionate pursuits"—and gratitude has been shown to decrease suicidal thoughts, independent of depression symptoms.

THE EVOLUTION OF GIVING

The evidence indicates that we are wired to give. Something positive is triggered inside of us when we give. While receiving gifts may make us happy, giving makes life more meaningful.

Vampire bats and Canada geese reveal why showing compassion is also evolutionarily beneficial. While Darwinism may be known for survival of the fittest, many psychologists, such as Dr. Dacher Keltner, have noted that survival doesn't necessarily involve violence and selfishness. Author of *Born to Be Good: The Science of a Meaningful Life*, Keltner notes that studies inspired by Darwin have shown that our capacity for play, caring, reverence, and modesty is built into our brains, bodies, genes, and social practices and is necessary for cooperative living.[7]

In a wonderful two-part series written for my blog, Dr. Greg Evans, a positive psychologist who directs the Happiness Enhancement Group, explains why giving makes us feel good.[8] He touches on this evolutionary aspect of giving and illustrates his points with two interesting examples from the animal world.

You might be familiar with the sight of Canada geese flying south in a V shape. The strongest flyers take turns leading the group where the air is most resistant. At the same time, if any of the birds fall behind the group, two other birds typically do as well in order to encourage the lagging bird to rejoin the group. This action increases the birds' chances of survival because others will help them if they fall behind. Dr. Evans also cites a study by Gerald S. Wilkinson that shows that vampire bats on a successful night of blood sucking will share their bounty with peers—another example of how altruism is important for the survival of a group.

These findings extend to the human species, as it has been found that we will punish those who do not show kindness. In one study, Werner Guth gave $20 to participants and instructed them to split the money with a partner. They could decide how much to share, but if the partners weren't happy with how much money they were given, they could refuse the cash and prevent the first participant from getting any money. On average, partners refused offers below $7. Perceived selfishness, then, is not rewarded.

Is it no wonder that kindness is a desirable trait in romantic partners? And what about businesses? According to the 2013 Cone Communications Social Impact Study, more than nine in ten Americans look to companies that support social or environmental issues in some way, and 88 percent want to hear from companies about those efforts.[9] A full 91 percent of American consumers want to see more products, services, and retailers support worthy causes. It's no surprise that Americans trust and have a more positive image of companies that give back.

It seems, then, that meaningful giving makes us happier while also making people want to be associated with us, personally and professionally. Good begets good. When this happens, everyone benefits, from the giver and the socially conscious business to the recipients of the good deed.

THE PATH TO MEANINGFUL GIVING

In the last chapter, I mentioned my desire to give back in a more meaningful way. I wrote about this on my blog in 2011, and it is still true today. I've thought about my journey toward living more philanthropically—which is a continuous journey, I might add. The more ways I find to give, the more I want to give. *But, why? Why am I never satisfied?* It could be that I simply haven't found that perfect giving strategy whose actions and results leave me feeling fulfilled.

Now that we understand some of the psychology behind giving and why we have that pull to give, you might be asking yourself, how does one get to the point of making life more meaningful? As I noted in the beginning of this chapter, some giving situations aren't as fulfilling as others. The nature of the giving makes a difference. Elizabeth Dunn and Michael Norton, authors of *Happy Money: The Science of Happier Spending*, suggest three ways for people to get the most out of their giving: choice, connection, and impact.[10]

We want to give, but we get the most satisfaction from giving when it is our choice. So being pressured into buying those high-priced candles or magazine subscriptions to support the school or scout troop of your coworker's child isn't going to rank high in meaningful giving. Giving in this environment can feel like an obligation. Researchers Netta Weinstein and Richard Ryan found that students who kept a daily diary felt better on days they did something to help another person or a worthy cause, but only if it was their choice. In contrast, prosocial behaviors that they felt they had to do did not make them feel as happy. When people are presented with options to help others, this empowers them to make a decision and feel satisfied with their giving, much like my son picking out Christmas gifts for a child in need.

Connections with our gifts are important as well. Research has shown that people are happier when they spend money on those they have closer ties to (such as significant others, close friends, and immediate family members) than those they have weaker ties to (like a friend of a friend or a step-uncle). As I noted in the Starbucks gift card example, the combination of investing in and spending time with the recipient of your giving provides the most happiness. Connections can also be made with complete strangers when, for example, donors are given the opportunity to read stories and see exactly the kind of impact that a gift can make. Donors create an emotional connection and stronger ties when they can actually interact with recipients through thank-you cards and other correspondence. I know I give more to those organizations that take the time to call, or send handwritten notes or personal e-mails directly to me, letting me know how my actions are making a difference. I feel like I am part of the solution, even if I am just a small piece of the impact puzzle.

Speaking of impact, the more specific a gift is, the better. People like to know exactly what their money is buying in the case of donations. So it makes sense that people experience a bigger boost in happiness when donating to campaigns like Spread the Net, which sends a mosquito net to sub-Saharan Africa for just $10, versus contributing to a bigger nonprofit organization like UNICEF. While both recipients are certainly worthy of support, it can be hard to see where your $10 will go in such a large organization. Research has also shown that when given money to spend however they choose, people will choose to spend the money on others rather than themselves when they've reflected on giving in the past. Remembering the emotional benefits of past giving is enough to make people want to give again.

Going back to my new definition of philanthropy, I noted in Chapter One that to give back in a meaningful way, a person should genuinely want to make a positive impact and act in a way that benefits someone or something else. I suspect that if you are reading this book, you have the first component covered. Those who want to give for more selfish reasons probably aren't looking for new giving models or putting much thought into a giving strategy. I hope the second component makes more sense in the context of what we've discussed—there's much more to giving than the traditional act of donating money to a charity that you may or may not have any personal connection to.

The next few chapters will focus on the specific giving models you can use in whole or in part to give in a meaningful way that makes sense for you.

WHAT HAPPENED WHEN I SHARED MY SMILE FOR THIRTY DAYS[II]

One weekend morning, as I sipped my coffee and scrolled through Twitter on my phone, I came across The Smile Epidemic's feed. Their bio at the time caught my eye: "Lend me your smile and I'll give it back to you with interest. Help us to start an epidemic :)"

I immediately knew that I needed to feature them for my Philanthropy Friday series. I contacted Jim Moss, the "smile guy" himself, to find out what he was doing over there in Canada.

The Smile Epidemic's mission is "to use our expertise in the field of positive psychology to educate others about the benefits of practicing expressed gratitude in an effort to increase overall mental health and well-being." Their goal is to create the "happiest community on Earth" by sharing what makes us happy.

The concept is simple. The Smile Epidemic wants you to be mindful of the simple things in life that bring you happiness. By taking note of those little things that make you smile for thirty days in a row and posting a picture of yourself on their website with a note in front of your smile, you can change the way you look at the world. A public gratitude journal, if you will.

Over the phone, Jim told me, "Simple things make a big difference." He noted that if we appreciate the simple things, we can erode the bad.

This epidemic started when Jim, a former lacrosse player, became ill. He had difficulty walking and discovered he had a muscular neurological disorder. At one point, he had to learn how to walk all over again—certainly not a positive time in a former high-level athlete's life.

From then on, any time his legs would start bothering him, he would wonder how much the disease would progress. His mind went straight to the worst-case scenario.

But something happened that changed his perspective on his disease and his life. He heard the sound of his kids laughing in the bathtub down the hall as he worked on a paper for his psychology class.

It was then that Jim realized that he should be thankful that he could hear this wonderful, happy sound. The fact that he wasn't in the hospital was something to be happy about. Because he didn't have time to write in his gratitude journal, he took a picture of himself holding up a piece of paper with a smile drawn across it. He posted it on Facebook and went back to his studies.

He took a few of these smile pictures after that night and continued to post them on Facebook. He found that people really enjoyed the pictures and started to send back their own photos. And that's when The Smile Epidemic was born.

It was a pivotal moment in his recovery process when Jim realized that he could focus on the many things he still had to be grateful for rather than on the things that he didn't have. By making his gratitude journal public through social media, Jim inspired others to exercise gratitude, too.

After my conversation with Jim, I started my own thirty days of happiness. It's one thing to hear about the effects of an online gratitude journal, but it's another to actually experience it. Because of all the photo taking I had to do, I enlisted my oldest son to take many of the pictures for me. It was fun to have him involved with the process. He loved reading about what made me smile and often asked me what I would write about before I even had a chance to ask him to take my picture. We had some good conversations at the dinner table about the things that had made us happy during the day.

I can honestly say that I felt much happier after those thirty days. What I realized was that no matter what happened on any given day, there was always something to smile about. Always. And that's something I remember every time I'm having a bad day.

WHAT I LEARNED ABOUT GIVING ON THE GROUND IN NICARAGUA

In March 2014, I had the opportunity to travel to Nicaragua with WaterAid America to observe and learn about their water and sanitation programs. I was chosen for the trip because of my affiliation with Mom Bloggers for Social Good as well as my personal connection to the WaterAid America team in New York City. I had come to know a few members of their small team as a donor and writer for the Global Team of 200, a specialized group of social good mom bloggers who work with and write about nonprofit and NGO partners that focus on women and children.

As a "global coalition of moms who care," Mom Bloggers for Social Good offers opportunity for moms to use their voice and their social media influence to enact positive change. Select members are also identified to travel to developing countries to see the work of its partners on the ground. I was overjoyed to follow a few of my close blogger friends' travels through Indonesia, India, and South Africa as they shared in real time what they were experiencing. Seeing other moms' perspectives on the areas they visited and the needs they described was powerful. The fact that I knew the women made me feel even more connected.

My insight trip with WaterAid America was life-changing and impactful for several reasons. For one thing, it was the first time I had ever seen such an extreme level of poverty firsthand. I was told that the only nation living in greater poverty in the Western Hemisphere is Haiti. Our team, which included a Mexican photographer, a Canadian journalist, and WaterAid America's media and communications officer, traveled far beyond any tourist attraction in the country. With our home base in Bilwi (or Puerto Cabezas), we ventured out to several indigenous communities on the Caribbean side of

Nicaragua in a car we had to physically push in order to get started each morning.

Prior to our departure, WaterAid America took all the necessary steps to get our team prepared for the trip. I visited a local travel clinic and received the required vaccinations and antimalarial pills. I shopped for lightweight cotton clothing that would protect me from mosquitos and the sun while also keeping me cool, and I purchased the highest levels of sunscreen and DEET-filled bug spray. I bought a travel guide to Nicaragua for reference and didn't dare show anyone the waiver I had to sign in order to get my tickets and itinerary.

The journey to Nicaragua was an experience in and of itself—our plane was forced to return to the Atlanta airport due to issues with the radar. Our amazing flight crew implored us to hurry off the plane in order to board another, since our destination airport in Nicaragua closed at midnight. Once safely in the capital of Managua, we had to take a domestic flight across the country on a twelve-seater plane where seatbelts apparently were optional.

Transportation was certainly an obstacle during my one-week trip, and it became evident that the poorly maintained roads and lack of infrastructure were huge factors in the lack of access to clean water and sanitation. While I expected life to be very different in the country, I still didn't feel prepared. Our hotel in Bilwi had the luxury of running water, but we were reminded not to drink it or brush our teeth with it. My quick showers in the morning were cold. We were supplied with copious amounts of bottled water. One day, after a long morning "in community," we stopped for lunch at a local restaurant. We washed our hands using a bucket of water on the side of the building and watched as a staff person made several trips to a nearby well to pump water in more buckets for the kitchen.

My most memorable experience was spending a night at Linda's house in Auhya Tara. Linda was a graduate of Water-Aid's training program, which had taught her how to build, install, and maintain wells so that she could not only provide access to clean water and sanitation to her village but also make some extra income for her family. After working on the casings for a new well she was building at her neighbor's house, she made her family, her neighbor's kids, and our team lunch. She opened her home to us and showed us the crops she maintained on the other side of the river, which she accessed with a dugout canoe. Like many Nicaraguans in the indigenous communities, Linda had no electricity. The pour flush toilet was behind the house, and the well, a short walk away. We ate dinner in the dark with headlamps on and at night listened to a transistor radio, the only connection to the outside world.

Experiencing a taste of real Nicaraguan life was deeply moving for me. The things that WaterAid America had to do in order to make the trip work—coordinating travel, food, and water—seemed more daunting to me than setting up interviews with people in the community or visits to work sites. In the area where we stayed, fewer than 20 percent of people had access to water and basic sanitation. I shared this experience with friends, family members, and social media followers. We even hosted a highly successful Twitter chat in WaterAid's office in Bilwi on World Water Day. According to Mom Bloggers for Social Good, the week we were in Nicaragua generated 1,800 tweets, reaching 2 million Twitter accounts with more than 10 million impressions and nearly 300 interested bloggers.

My experience in Nicaragua showed me the power of giving in a very personal and meaningful way. If I had a choice of nonprofits to travel with, WaterAid was at the top. I was already writing about the need for universal access to water and sanitation, but my passion for the cause was deepened through the experience of living without that access for a week. And I could clearly see the impact I was making through the interactions I had in Nicaragua and with those who followed my trip online.

PUTTING IT ALL TOGETHER

In all of this, we have to remember that what makes one happy doesn't necessarily make another happy. Our choices and connections will all be different. The types of impact we want to make will be as diverse as our interests, talents, personalities, and backgrounds. Finding that meaningful life will be a different journey for us all. The good thing is that there are many ways in which we can give. We're about to explore six specific giving models. For extra inspiration, you'll find stories of how individuals and companies have successfully found meaning in their giving.

Before we dive into the giving models, you might want to measure where you are on the happiness scale as you begin your simple giving journey. You may also want to practice some actions that will help you create happiness through giving. Below you'll find some suggested action steps, based on the research discussed in this chapter. I've also included some resources, should you want to dig deeper into the world of positive psychology and the study of happiness.

THE PSYCHOLOGY OF GIVING:
ACTION STEPS TO GET YOU STARTED

1. *Think of Someone Who Has Done Something for You,
   Write Them a Thank-you Note, and Read It to Them*
   This act is suggested in Dr. Martin Seligman's TED talk on
   positive psychology, and can have a profound effect on both
   you and the recipient.

2. *Do Something Philanthropic with a Friend or Family
   Member*
   As noted earlier in this chapter, it feels better to serve along-
   side others.

3. *Perform a Random Act of Kindness for Someone Else*
   It feels good to perform kind acts, and your recipients will
   feel good, too. These connections will make you happier and
   hopefully create a domino effect of kindness.

4. *Take Note of What Makes You Smile and Share It on the
   Smile Epidemic (www.thesmileepidemic.com)*
   This online gratitude journal encourages sharing in order to
   promote positive thinking and create the happiest community on Earth.

5. *Help Out a Friend in Need*
   This gives you an opportunity to create a deeper connection

and practice compassion while letting a friend know that he or she is not alone.

THE PSYCHOLOGY OF GIVING: RESOURCES AND ASSESSMENTS

- Authentic Happiness (www.authentichappiness.sas.upenn .edu): The homepage of Dr. Martin Seligman, director of the Positive Psychology Center at the University of Pennsylvania and founder of positive psychology. The website includes resources and several questionnaires centered on character strengths and happiness.

- Take the Gross National Happiness Index survey at http:// survey.happycounts.org/user/signup: A collaborative project of the Happiness Initiative. This 10- to 15-minute survey is a self-assessment of your happiness and well-being.

- Read about the "10 Keys to Happier Living" from Action for Happiness (www.actionforhappiness.org/10-keys): Based on research in psychology and related fields, evidence suggests these ten keys consistently have a positive impact on people's happiness and well-being.

- Watch Martin Seligman's TED Talk on the new era of positive psychology (www.ted.com/talks/martin_seligman

_on_the_state_of_psychology.html): Filmed in 2004, Seligman talks about how modern psychology should move beyond a focus on disease.

- Greater Good Science Center (www.greatergood.berkeley.edu/education): Based at the University of California, Berkeley, the Greater Good Science Center's website is filled with useful information. Take quizzes, read about the latest research, and find resources about the science of living a meaningful life.

3 Giving Model 1: Everyday Acts of Kindness

*No act of kindness, no matter how small,
is ever wasted.*

Aesop

*Three things in human life are important.
The first is to be kind. The second is to be
kind. And the third is to be kind.*

Henry James

As we dive into our models of giving, we start with the simplest form of all. Kindness. Kindness is the simple quality of being considerate, friendly, and generous to others. An act of kindness can change the trajectory of your entire day, whether you are performing the act or on the receiving end. Think about how good it feels to have a friendly stranger give you a big smile while walking down the street or to help an elderly neighbor bring groceries into the house.

Performing random acts of kindness has become a popular activity and is particularly common after tragic events, reminding us to be more considerate of others. You may have heard stories of people helping strangers in natural disasters or paying for someone else's toll in honor of the victims of a heartbreaking event such as the shootings at Sandy Hook Elementary School. These acts of giving make sense when you consider them as a way of coping with the reality of such horrific and life-changing events. We are searching for meaning. We want reassurance that people are indeed humane.

The results of these kind actions are astounding because they often create a chain reaction. One person does something good, and the recipient of that good deed wants to pay it forward and do something kind for someone else. The kindness continues, whether the first person realizes it or not. That's where the fun comes in, because you often perform the act of kindness with the hope that you will make someone's day and that it will continue on from person to person. Who knows what kind of difference you can make in someone's life? It almost becomes a game.

Social scientists James Fowler and Nicholas Chistakis have shown that acts of generosity and kindness are indeed contagious.[1] Happiness can be spread, and if we are with people who are happy, their happiness rubs off on us.

To me, performing an act of kindness is a gateway that leads to more giving. Even if you're not ready to make a huge commitment, incorporating small, everyday acts of kindness into your life could lead you to bigger philanthropic endeavors. Your good deeds provide you with that rush of happiness when you give, and it doesn't take much time or effort to complete one.

The best thing about everyday acts of kindness is that you can perform them with little to no money. You can also easily incorporate these acts into your day. In fact, you may already be carrying out acts of kindness without realizing it. Here are some examples:

- Holding open a door for a stranger
- Allowing a busy mom with kids to cut in front of you in the checkout line (much appreciated!)
- Letting someone take a left turn in traffic
- Paying for a stranger's coffee at your local café
- Helping an older person load groceries into her car
- Bringing dinner over to a neighbor's house
- Delivering doughnuts to the local fire department (one of our favorites!)
- Picking up trash in your neighborhood
- Paying someone a compliment

- Writing a thank-you note
- Offering free babysitting to a couple or a single parent who could use a night out
- Smiling at strangers
- Donating used books (in good condition) to your local library

I could go on and on with examples of acts of kindness. And I have no doubt you could, too. It's no wonder these acts of kindness are contagious. They are easy and fun to do. It is often a surprisingly uplifting experience to be on the receiving end of a kind act. Have you ever been in the middle of a bad day and had a perfect stranger offer you a compliment? It doesn't happen often, but it has happened to me. I can tell you that my day was instantly better. Another fun part about kindness is that the deeds themselves are often anonymous. When you hear about a coffee shop that was hit with an avalanche of good people paying for other customers' orders, no one learns about the first person who put down the money to start the game. It doesn't matter, either. You simply enjoy the rush that comes with giving back.

Let's go back to our definition of *philanthropy* for a moment, since acts of kindness aren't always associated with the term. These acts fit our definition perfectly because they're motivated by the desire to make an impact—in this case, to simply make someone happier—and the act benefits someone else. Usually acts of kindness benefit individuals directly, but you could also affect whole organizations and causes. Taking the definition a step further, kind acts almost always inspire others to perform their own good deeds by "paying it forward," thus making the giving act sustainable over time—at least for a short period.

I hope you'll be inspired by the next few stories of everyday people and organizations that took their acts of kindness to the next level of giving.

400 ACTS OF KINDNESS TO CELEBRATE 100 DAYS[2]

Elementary schools around the United States often have celebrations and projects to commemorate the hundredth day of school. While I don't know the exact origin of these festivities, it is presumably a celebration of the halfway mark of the school year, which also allows younger kids to hone their counting skills.

In the past, my oldest son has had to collect a hundred items and put them on a poster board or in a bag to bring with him to school. With kindergartners and first graders, an emphasis is placed on number sense, place values, and counting. There has been a philanthropic twist to his hundredth day of school celebration in the past couple of years, as each grade in his school—four total—is challenged to perform one hundred acts of kindness.

Second, third, fourth, and fifth graders at Harriet Beecher Stowe Elementary School in Brunswick, Maine, must come up with at least a hundred donations for a local nonprofit. Assistant Principal Josh Levy tells me that the idea to add the giving component to the celebration came from the School Community Committee. The committee is composed of teachers, administrators, and support staff of the school and meets monthly to inspire and enhance greater school community. Because the school is large, the goal is to bring students and faculty together. With such a large community, the goal of collecting a hundred donations per class is easily attainable. The committee also helps coordinate food donations during the holidays.

In the past, the school has worked with the local animal shelter, a hunger prevention program, a homeless shelter, and a teen center in town. Parents receive a flyer listing items that each nonprofit needs most. Special-needs students keep track of the donations and through handmade charts show how close the classes are to their goal. These students are natural leaders for the hundred-days celebration, as they practice kindness each week, collecting and tracking donations and writing about it in their gratitude journals.

In 2014, the school successfully donated more than six hundred items—far surpassing their original goal. Not surprisingly, the local nonprofits were grateful for the participation and donations of the students and staff at the elementary school, often thanking the students personally for their generosity when they picked up items. In addition, the students were able to work together to reach a goal for a good cause.

1,OOO MITZVAHS[3] (WWW.IOOOMITZVAHS.ORG)

The book *1,000 Mitzvahs: How Small Acts of Kindness Can Heal, Inspire, and Change Your Life*, by Linda Cohen, is about a project Linda took on after the death of her father. She set out to perform one thousand mitzvahs in her father's memory. She told me, "Though a mitzvah is actually a commandment in Judaism, it has also become synonymous for doing acts of kindness."

Linda didn't set out to change the world. She simply wanted to perform acts of kindness to honor her father. She found that the cumulative effect of the project not only helped her in her grieving but also had a huge positive impact on her life.

Each chapter has a different theme—such as food, volunteer work, donations, environmental conscience, birthdays, death and grieving—and includes short stories about the mitzvahs performed. Over the course of the project, Linda realized how easy it was to do good deeds, and she began to notice when others did good deeds as well. She chronicled her mitzvahs on her blog and continues to post mitzvahs on her Facebook page.

Her mitzvahs included things like making sure the next person in the public bathroom had toilet paper, using reusable shopping bags on vacation, acknowledging someone who had done a good job, taking the time to send handwritten thank-you notes, and telling people about how they had positively impacted her. These are simple acts that we can do every day and put a smile on other people's faces.

Linda's husband and kids participated in the project as well, even discussing whether or not certain acts counted as a mitzvah. The book illustrates how performing mitzvahs, or "spontaneous kindness" as Linda describes it, helped the entire family give more.

Since its release in 2011, *1,000 Mitzvahs* has inspired others to take on their own mitzvah projects. Linda has spoken at several elementary and high schools that have created their own versions of the project. In addition, several synagogues have taken on mitzvah projects, and one church pastor asked his congregants to perform mitzvahs instead of giving something up for Lent. The ripple effect of the book has been felt across the globe as well. A girl as far away as Australia was inspired by the book to perform mitzvahs and to get her community involved for her bat mitzvah celebration.

GOOD DEEDS AT BAD DOG DELI

A funny thing started to happen during the summer of 2014 at Bad Dog Deli, a sandwich shop in Scarborough, Maine. A customer would come into the deli early in the morning and leave extra money with the person at the register. The only instruction left with the money was, "Pay it forward!"

As owner Benjamin Grant describes it, the amount of money left with the restaurant would be anywhere from $5 to $20. Months later, the tradition continues. It isn't always the same person who does the kind act, but it almost always happens early in the morning.

The staff at Bad Dog Deli typically passes the money on to the next person that comes in line. They explain the concept of paying it forward when the money is used on that customer. On some days, the small amount of $5 would actually last the entire day. People would take from the money as necessary or add to the pot as they were able to afford. Bad Dog Deli has thanked the people who have paid it forward for giving them the "opportunity to spread the kindness and humanity they possess."

"I have always thought this to be a great and easy way to give, and the people receiving it seem to feel the same way!" explains Benjamin. Though Bad Dog Deli hasn't had a day when the money carries over to the next, they have had customers who benefited from the kind act come back to the restaurant a few days later to start a new pot of money with which to pay forward. The returning recipients remarked how good it felt for someone else to buy their lunch and so they wanted to return the favor for the next person.

KINDSPRING (WWW.KINDSPRING.ORG)

KindSpring, a project of ServiceSpace, is a website dedicated to fostering and celebrating small acts of anonymous kindness around the world. To date, KindSpring has more than 63,000 members in its community, who have more than 72,000 kindness stories and have shipped more than one million Smile Cards all over the world.

The concept for KindSpring came about in 2003 when a young college student wondered what it would be like if, instead of hazing, we pranked people with acts of kindness. Instead of humiliating others, what if we put a smile on their faces? Smile Cards were created soon thereafter. Small enough to fit in a pocket, these simple cards had the word *Smile* printed on them. The cards also included a note that informed the recipient that they were "tagged" by an anonymous act of kindness and were invited to pay it forward by doing something kind for someone else. The website, then called Help Others, was created as a space where people could share their anonymous acts of kindness with a community and find inspiration in the stories of others. People can also order or print out their own Smile Cards, which are available in several different languages.

According to Arathi Ravichandran, one of the almost fifty volunteers who run KindSpring's website, the idea is to leverage technology in order to inspire others with small acts of kindness. In that sense, KindSpring provides an easy way for its community to amplify the power of generosity. When people sign up for the site, they are given aliases, keeping members and stories anonymous. No one knows who has performed the acts of kindness reported on KindSpring, making one wonder if someone down the street or across the world might be the perpetrator of a good deed.

A newer feature of KindSpring is the 21-Day Challenge, where participants are encouraged to perform a unique act of kindness each day for twenty-one days in a row. Doing something consistently for three weeks helps to form a habit, while participating with a group fosters bonding and creates shared values. Each challenge focuses on a specific theme ranging from kindness to mindfulness. According to volunteer Audrey Lin, the 21-Day Challenge was created to support people who wanted to invest in their own microcommunities such as companies, schools, families, churches, and groups of friends. However, anyone can join an existing challenge or host his own challenge.

The KindSpring platform is completely ad-free and volunteer run, as are the other projects on ServiceSpace, which runs on three basic operating principles. The organization chooses not to fund-raise so that it can serve with whatever resources it currently has and does not worry about asking people for money. Being founded by volunteers, ServiceSpace also aims to remain all volunteer run. Finally, ServiceSpace focuses on taking small steps—we can't change the world unless we change ourselves and create a ripple effect around us.

Other ServiceSpace projects include DailyGood (www .dailygood.org), an uplifting news site; KarmaTube (www .karmatube.org), a collection of inspiring videos; Karma Kitchen (www.karmakitchen.org), a pay-it-forward restaurant; Conversations (www.conversations.org), a collection of in-depth interviews with artists; and Awakin (www.awakin.org), a curated source of secular wisdom.

ARK PROJECT NOW (WWW.ARKPROJECTNOW.COM)

Alex Radelich's life changed when he decided to watch the movie *Evan Almighty* one day at the end of finals in his dorm room at Purdue University. Though he had seen the movie before, the end connected with him deeply that day. In the movie, Steve Carell's character asks, "How can we change the world?" Morgan Freeman, who plays the role of God in the movie, replies "One act of random kindness at a time." At that moment in the film, "God" writes the letters A R K— an abbreviation for "Act of Random Kindness"—into the sand with a stick.

It was then that Alex started to question what he was doing with his life. He wanted to lead by example and create smiles along the way. He made a video from his room that explained his idea to spread kindness around the world by doing things like holding doors for people or paying for someone's order in a coffee shop. In the video, he asked if anyone wanted to join him in his kindness endeavor. Alex posted the video on social media, figuring it would be seen by only a few of his friends.

Except the video went viral. Within twenty-four hours of posting it, he heard from people as far away as Russia. From there, Alex sold some of his personal belongings, had some ARK cards made—which tell people they have been hit with an act of random kindness and encourage them to pay it forward—and started a website for his kindness project.

In the first year, Alex and his friends went out of their way to be kind and posted their deeds on social media. When they raised $2,000 in thirteen days, just a few weeks before Christmas, to help victims of a fire, they realized they could do much more.

Alex dropped out of college and went full force with his project from there. He told me of a time when he and his best friend, Dalton, had talked for two hours about their dreams for the future and came up with the road trip idea for ARK Project Now. They decided to find a way to fund a trip that would take them 6,000 miles in an RV around the country. Their goal was to inspire an epidemic of kindness and raise one kind pledge per mile.

They figured they'd need about $5,000–$10,000 to fund their acts of kindness and $5,000 for living expenses. In February of 2014, ARK Project Now received its 501(c)(3) nonprofit status. They raised the first $6,000 through a local event at a Ford dealership that supported nonprofits. After a month of promoting a video entry into KIND Causes, a venture of KIND Health Snacks that supports individuals and organizations that are working to make the world kinder, ARK Project Now was awarded an additional $10,000 in funding. Alex, Dalton, and three of their friends found themselves an RV next, selling advertising on the side of the vehicle to help pay for it.

From June 4 to July 18, 2014, the friends traveled through more than a dozen states, spreading kindness along the way and documenting their journey online. One of the most memorable experiences was when they visited the Rainbow House in Omaha, Nebraska, where families from out of town are given accommodations while their loved ones receive treatment at a nearby children's hospital. They cooked food for the families staying at the house and bonded with the McGee family, whose child was being treated for a heart condition. They later took the family on a shopping spree at Target.

Theodore Thatcher, another one of Alex's friends and ARK Project Now team member, says one of the most beautiful parts of the project is the experience everyone involved has when they participate. "Whether you're the ARKer, or the ARKed, you have been a part of a human exchange, a communication of value that has become all too rare. Having a premeditated structure that facilitates charity is commendable, but choosing a lifestyle that owns a core value of kindness is unstoppable. We believe living this way is catalytic."

The mission behind ARK Project Now is to create a community of passionate, outgoing people who consciously decide to make kindness a habit. Alex envisions the website as a tool for creating a kindness movement and active community where people share their own good stories. He wants ARK Project Now to be the "voice of light." On the website, www .arkprojectnow.com, people can pledge to "Just Do One" ARK per day, week, or month. Users of the site can also share their own stories of how they have impacted others or been impacted by kindness. You can follow their adventures on the ARK Project Now blog and other social media.

KIND HEALTHY SNACKS (WWW.KINDSNACKS.COM)

KIND Healthy Snacks has a social mission to make the world a little kinder through acts big and small. Though you may recognize KIND for its bright packaging and tasty snacks with ingredients you can recognize and pronounce, their message of "holistic kindness" has been the foundation of the business since its inception.

Founder and CEO Daniel Lubetzky refers to KIND as a not-ONLY-for-profit company. The inspiration for building compassion into his business came from Daniel's father, who survived the Holocaust thanks to several acts of kindness. Hearing firsthand stories from his father inspired Daniel to develop sustainable, socially driven companies that strive to better our world. With success came a much more demanding schedule and a growing frustration over the lack of healthy, tasty, and convenient snack choices to fuel his busy lifestyle. This, coupled with his concern about the rising obesity and diabetic epidemic in America, ultimately drove Daniel to launch KIND in 2004.

The mission to inspire kindness has progressed over the years for Daniel and KIND. When the company first launched, the staff were the protagonists. They were the ones going out giving massages and carrying other people's groceries. These acts progressed to "KIND Tuesdays," where the company would send out a specific kindness mission, such as giving a note of thanks to someone who inspired you. If enough people reported doing the act of kindness, KIND would reward the achievement by investing in an even greater act of kindness, such as cleaning up a local beach.

Today, KIND wants to empower its community to make kindness a habit and a priority. KIND Causes awards grants to people who spread kindness in whatever way makes sense to them. ARK Project Now was just one example of a KIND Cause winner. Winners are also supported in nonfinancial ways, through product donations, mentorship, and publicity in the media. A signature "KIND activation" is the flower wall, where individuals are invited to pick a flower and pass it on to someone else—a friend, loved one, teacher, coworker, or even a stranger. The flower wall serves as a fun way to get people to try KIND products, but also acts as a reminder to spread kindness through small actions every day.

Anyone with a Twitter or Instagram account can celebrate and share kindness by using the hashtag #kindawesome. The captured experiences become part of a larger living mural on the #kindawesome homepage (www.kindsnacks.com/kindawesome). KIND also hands out #kindawesome cards to those spotted doing an act of kindness for someone else. The cards can be redeemed online for a sample of KIND snacks as a "thank-you." Two are given so that the recipient can pay it forward when they see another person performing an act of kindness.

As far as impact goes, KIND recognizes how hard it is to measure kindness. Instead of counting product donations, they look at the number of kind acts performed, facilitated, or celebrated. To date, more than a million kind acts have been completed through the KIND Movement community.

MAKING IT HAPPEN

As we have seen in this chapter, everyday events in one's life may inspire kindness. Linda performed mitzvahs to help her get through the grieving process after the loss of her father. Alex found himself questioning where he was going with his life after watching a movie and found answers once he started to incorporate kindness into his normal routine. The founders of KindSpring looked to take the act of hazing and turn it onto its head by "pranking" people with kindness. Harriet Beecher Stowe Elementary School saw an opportunity to bring its larger school community together by making good deeds a central part of a school celebration.

The stories in this chapter also make it clear that being the recipient of simple acts of everyday kindness can inspire others to perform their own good deeds. Bad Dog Deli and other restaurants around the country have seen how one act of kindness, in paying for a person's order, can last for hours as customers continue to pay the kindness forward to the next customer. The CEO of KIND Healthy Snacks was inspired by the acts of kindness that helped his father survive the Holocaust.

To encourage the kindness to continue, KindSpring and ARK Project Now give people a forum to share their kindness stories online and hand out cards as a reminder to recipients to pay kindness forward. Ben's staff at Bad Dog Deli takes the time to explain the act of kindness a stranger has provided to their customers. Linda wrote a book and continues to share her inspiration for mitzvahs on social media and in talks. KIND awards grants to support kindness and fosters a community through its #kindawesome hashtag. While acts of kindness are often completed anonymously, sharing and acknowledging kindness around you has a powerful effect on people. Positive change is contagious. You not only feel good making kindness an everyday occurrence but you also have the opportunity to give that same feeling to others. Who knows what kind of effect you can have on someone's life—or your own—through simple everyday acts of kindness.

EVERYDAY ACTS OF KINDNESS: ACTION STEPS TO GET YOU STARTED

At this point in the chapter, your brain should already be reeling with ideas for everyday acts of kindness. The best part about this giving model is that it is easy for anyone of any age to carry out. Here are just a few quick suggestions for action steps to get you started, followed by additional resources to help you carry out your acts.

1. *Get into a Kindness Mind-set*

    Sometimes we go through our day without putting much thought into our actions beyond what we absolutely have to do next. Take some time to think about ways to incorporate kindness into your day. It's as easy as letting a car go in front of you during the morning commute or opening the door for a stranger. ARK Project Now places emphasis on the idea of "Just Do One." Pledging to do just one act of kindness a day and challenging others to do the same can have a large impact in spreading kindness.

2. *Find Some Kindness Cards*

    When you perform an act of kindness, leave a card behind so that others know they are the recipients of kindness. The card should encourage the recipient to keep the kindness going by performing his or her own act. Actually, leave two cards so the next person can easily pay it forward as well. It's like a game of tag.

3. *Put Some Coffee on the Wall*

    Not literally, of course. The idea here is to buy an additional coffee (or something like coffee) and ask the cashier to put the extra coffee "on the wall" for someone who does not have the money to purchase a coffee themselves. It's a fun act of kindness that can have a lasting ripple effect.

4. *Become a RAKtivist*

   A RAKtivist promotes kindness in his or her community by walking the walk instead of just talking the talk. You can join more than 1,600 RAKtivists by filling out a simple online application on the Random Acts of Kindness website (www.randomactsofkindness.org/raktivists). Perks include a private Facebook group full of other kindness-minded people and monthly social media and community kindness raids.

5. *Share Your Kindness*

   Once you perform your act of kindness, see if you can find a way to share the act with others. The idea is to inspire others to do their own good deeds. You might post something on social media or share a story on one of the websites listed in the resources section below. Document your progress as you take this journey, and let the world see how you change through the process.

6. *Apply for a Kindness Grant*

   Do you have a big idea to spread kindness that could use some funding to get started or to continue? Head on over to KIND Causes (causes.kindsnacks.com) and apply for a grant. You will need to create a cause that can be voted on by the KIND community. Funding is awarded throughout the year to different causes.

EVERYDAY ACTS OF KINDNESS: RESOURCES

Get into a Kindness Mind-set

- The Random Acts of Kindness Foundation (www.random actsofkindness.org/kindness-ideas): The Random Acts of Kindness Foundation offers a collection of kindness ideas that can be filtered by category, cost, and time investment. There are also specific lesson plans, kindness project ideas, and other resources for educators available on this website (www.randomactsofkindness.org/educators).

- KindSpring.org (KindSpring.org/ideas): With "oodles" of kindness ideas, KindSpring allows you to search for kindness ideas by themes such as friends and family, environment, under $5, at work, special occasions, and more. You can even suggest your own kindness idea.

- Simple Ways to Give Back List (www.favepages.com/list /anotherjennifer/simple-ways-to-give-every-day): This curated list, hosted on FavePages, offers up some inspiration for simple ways to give back through acts of kindness. You can also add your own suggestion to the list, share it on social media, and even embed it on a blog or website.

- The Kindness Project (www.thekindproject.org/kindness
  -stories.html): Started by a college student disenchanted
  with environmental politics and in need of inspiration, the
  Kindness Project is a collection of audio stories on kindness. Brooke Welty collected the stories in 2012 as she traveled the country by bus and train and interviewed people
  about kindness from coast to coast.

- ARK Project Now Pledge (www.arkprojectnow.com/commit
  -to-one): Take ARK Project Now's pledge to "do just one"
  act of kindness per day, per week, or per month. You decide
  what kindness looks like, and no act is too small.

Find Some Kindness Cards

- Smile Cards (www.kindspring.org/smilecards/): Smile Cards
  from KindSpring have the word *Smile* printed on them with a
  note that tells the recipient they have been "tagged" and are
  now "it" to encourage paying it forward. You can request pre-
  printed cards from the website or download and print them
  out yourself.

- Kindness Cards (www.kindnesscards.org): At the cost of
  $10 for five cards, Kindness Cards feature a unique code.
  When entered on the website, the code allows the recipient
  to tell the story of how he or she received the card. It also

gives the recipient ideas on how to pay it forward to someone else.

Share Your Kindness

- KindSpring Stories (www.kindspring.org/story): KindSpring features anonymous stories of kindness from around the world. Read them to get inspired and share your own story.
- ARK Project Now Stories (www.arkprojectnow.com/share -your-story): ARK Project Now shares their stories of kindness on their blog and other social media. They want to hear how you've impacted and been impacted by those around you.
- Random Acts of Kindness Foundation Stories (www.ran domactsofkindness.org/kindness-stories/share-your-story): The Random Acts of Kindness Foundation allows you to share your kindness stories, whether you are a participant, observer, or recipient of a kind act.

4 Giving Model 2: A New Approach to Traditional Philanthropy

We make a living by what we get, but we make a life by what we give.

Winston Churchill

When you hear the word *philanthropy*, what comes to mind? Most often, it's money. Donating money, to be more specific. As mentioned previously, a search on Google gives me the definition "the desire to promote the welfare of others, expressed especially by the generous donation of money to good causes." While philanthropy is most often associated with giving money, I would put volunteering time to a nonprofit as a close second, in terms of what people associate with philanthropy.

I hear a lot of people say they don't donate or volunteer on a regular basis because they either don't think about it or don't feel like they have enough money or time to give in order to make a difference. I'm guilty of using both excuses. As I mentioned earlier, I learned to combat these barriers by starting my own public giving pledge. While not quite the well-known giving pledges made by billionaires, these public commitments held me accountable for actively seeking and investing in a different charity each month. I gave what I could and didn't disclose the amount of my donations.

I learned some key lessons during the first year of my giving pledge in 2012.[1] I was more likely to give to causes where I had a personal connection because I could see the impact of my donation firsthand. If I wrote about a nonprofit and interviewed someone from the organization for a blog post, I was more compelled to donate. Of course, I would also donate on a whim when I felt the immediate need to help, usually after tragedies such as a large-scale fire that happened in my community. I donated immediately to the local Red Cross. I also found that the more tangible gifts were the most meaningful ones I gave over the year. I can immediately recall, for example, the donation I made to WaterAid America that paid for four faucets to provide clean, safe water to areas that lack sanitation. I also contributed to microloans that helped women start new businesses and new lives for their families. As far as ongoing contributions go, personal responses from the nonprofits I gave to made a big difference in terms of making me want to donate again. A handwritten note or personal e-mail to say thank-you meant a lot to me after I made a donation.

The most important lesson I learned from my giving pledge was that once I made donating a priority in my life, it became a habit. I did not have a problem finding organizations to send money to. In fact, I often found the donation ideas would just come to me, somehow, each month. After a while, I didn't have to do much thinking about where my donation would end up, and I almost never had to remind myself of my pledge. I have since stopped writing about every donation I make because I felt like it was too much. The experiment worked well for me, and I believe it inspired others to think more about giving to charity. I started to feel like I was oversharing about my giving and that it was better to focus on the stories of good causes and let my readers decide on their own how they would like to support them.

The other barrier to philanthropy—I will stick to using the word *barrier* and not *problem*—is that people often don't know how or where to give. As a professional working in non-profit development, I've actually had to say no to donations because while the intentions to give were good, the donors were giving items the organization did not need. I would then have to redirect their giving intention into something more useful to the organization, which was often money to pay for something that was specifically needed. Even the richest people in the world have trouble giving. Many have said it is easier to make money than to give it.

There are some new buzzwords around philanthropy that have emerged in the past couple of years. *Philanthro-teen* describes young, empowered girls who have a sense of purpose and responsibility around giving. I first heard of this term at the 2013 Social Good Summit in New York City. Under the influence of their giving parents and those around them, kids are giving earlier and earlier and in simple ways such as picking up trash and donating money. Children embrace giving quickly because it empowers them to help other people in a very tangible and simple way. My elementary school–aged son is proud to collect Box Tops for Education labels and recyclable bottles and cans to support his school. He also knows that when he volunteers with me for our local BackPack Program, he is helping to feed his less fortunate peers over the weekend. Developing these personal connections to giving early on can only help kids become more philanthropic as adults.

Another term I have heard is *philanthropreneur*, describing one who uses "practical and entrepreneurial approaches to the pursuit of philanthropy."[2] While it is a term reserved more for those with a good deal of money, such as Virgin's Sir Richard Branson or AOL's Steve Case, it infers that entrepreneurs have an obligation to give more as they make more and use their smart business sense to do so.

The mere existence of these philanthropic buzzwords tells us that people have the pull to give more. The rates of giving in America tell us the same thing. According to Philanthropy .com, while those who earned $200,000 or more decreased their giving to charity by 4.6 percent from 2006 to 2012, low- and middle-income families increased their giving.[3] Those who make less than $100,000 increased their percentage of income given to charity by 4.5 percent in the same time period, despite earning less. Historically, those who make less tend to give the highest percentage of their income.

But where do you start? And if you are already giving regularly, how do you know you are making the most impact with your gifts? Could you give more? And to whom or for what cause? These are all legitimate questions to have running through your brain. *Transparency* is a term that is heard a lot in relation to nonprofit organizations. People want to know where their money is going and how it will be spent. The following stories will give you some insight on how to approach philanthropy in a new way—that is, more than just writing a check at the end of the year for a tax deduction.

RUTH RIDDICK: BECOMING
A NONPROFIT PHILANTHROPIST

"Philanthropy? That's money, right?" Well, not exactly . . .

Five years ago, when Ruth Riddick joined the board of directors for a Maine nonprofit with a mission very close to her heart, she thought philanthropy was about writing checks, which was always a challenge in the shaky freelance economy in which she works. Sure, she'd gladly share her relevant experience and talents, and she was delighted to make time to prepare for meetings and attend events, but she was still worried that she wouldn't be able to meet the organization's "philanthropy" goals.

Ruth decided to explore what her role in the nonprofit world should be.

Researching current trends on the Internet, Ruth found Andrea McManus, a widely respected expert in nonprofit governance who advises that we need to change the mind-set that equates *philanthropy* with *fund-raising*. She says philanthropy is much bigger, and is, in fact, the single most significant driver in the nonprofit sector. McManus's provocative message is simply that "philanthropy is the individual's investment in the social good achieved by the nonprofit." So social good should be clearly signaled in the organization's mission statement, and, ideally, the investment should be shared by the entire organizational community—board, executives, staff, and volunteers. The specifics of our contribution are going to be determined by our role, skills, and availability.

"If you're invested and participating in the organization's mission, you're a philanthropist," McManus said. Ruth found this message to be something she could get behind. She also cites a quote from an article I wrote on reframing philanthropy: "Our dedication to the organization, and our belief in the mission and social good of the work that is done every day, are our investment."[4] According to this definition, all of our actions as board members count as philanthropic, whether or not there is any cash involved.

Of course, there's also a financial dimension to supporting nonprofit missions, a process which, according to McManus, also includes strategic, big-picture development, donor cultivation for long-term sustainability, and inevitably, fund-raising.

"Just bringing up the subject of philanthropy can lead to defensiveness and fear," says Emily Semenchuk, forward-thinking board president at Crossroads, a Scarborough, Maine–based nonprofit providing addiction treatment services. "Talking about money is something that is culturally frowned upon," although she also encourages us to open up our attitudes.

Part of a new generation of nonprofit leaders, Semen-chuk encourages nonprofits to aim for full philanthropic participation—including an appropriate annual donation—from all members of the organizational community. Increasingly, this paradigm is what donors and grant makers are looking to see in the organizations they are funding. We're well advised to follow Semenchuk's suggestion.

Meanwhile, Ruth wonders, as I have, how many people hold back from giving because they think they can't make a difference? Today, Ruth feels liberated in seeing her philanthropic commitment in every aspect of her work, even if it is in stuffing five hundred envelopes and leaving a $5 check.

GIVING CIRCLES FUND

(WWW.GIVINGCIRCLESFUND.ORG)

The Giving Circles Fund's mission is to inspire a lifelong habit of philanthropy by empowering communities to give together. Formerly known as the One Percent Foundation, the organization was created when its two founders, Mike and Daniel, calculated that they were giving less than 1 percent of what they were bringing in for income in 2007. In graduate school at the time, Mike and Daniel were shocked because they had considered themselves to be philanthropic people.

They decided to get some friends together and start pooling their money.

The first giving circle they created had about thirty people in it. They decided as a committee who would benefit from their donations. While they never intended to start an organization, three years later they found themselves with a circle of one hundred donors around the country and in need of an executive director. Lana Volftsun was hired to help manage the growing giving circle.

Seeing how Mike and Daniel's giving circle caught on with friends and friends of friends, Lana's idea was to create a website for the project, building an online giving circle platform that anyone could join for free. Lana also added the opportunity for people to create their own giving circles. One Percent Foundation became the Giving Circles Fund at the beginning of 2014. The vision for the fund is to build an inclusive movement of thoughtful, committed philanthropists.

Today, there are several different giving circles available to join that range in size from five to a hundred people. Some circles are cause-based, while others are city-based. Some giving circles meet in person to discuss how their funds will be used, while others do business strictly online.

It is free to become a member of the Giving Circles Fund. Once you become a member, there are options to join private and public circles, or you can start your own circle. The minimum donation for members is $10 per month. Anyone who is part of a giving circle can nominate a nonprofit to be the recipient of the pooled money. Everyone in the circle votes on who receives the final grant. Grants are awarded annually, semiannually, or quarterly, depending on the circle.

Because the Giving Circles Fund caters mostly to Millennials, or those in their twenties and thirties, the organization also provides philanthropic training to its members. According to Lana, most of the members who join have never given before, making such training a key element to success. Many members didn't initially feel they could make an impact and didn't know where to give. Evaluating which nonprofits to give to is also a daunting task. The training helps circle members assess the causes that are nominated and the impact that can be made. The goal is for members to learn to be both consistent and strategic in their giving, understanding what questions to ask during the process.

Most members give about $10 to $30 per month and vote on grants in the amount of $10,000 to $25,000. The Giving Circles Fund does not take any percentage of the donations, so members know that all the money they give will go to the chosen nonprofit. As a 501(c)(3) organization itself, the Giving Circles Fund relies on "tips" from members when they join, along with traditional fund-raising. According to Lana, about 70 percent of its generous members tip the fund. There is also a paid option to create corporate giving circles. These Pro Giving Circles have additional benefits that enable an organization to create collective giving within the company while also strengthening its community.

Just about two years after its inception, the Giving Circles Fund boasted 250 members, 40 circles, and $400,000 raised for nonprofits. Ideally, Lana says, she wants to see members have a meaningful experience for one to two years within a giving circle, find an organization they love, and "graduate" by consistently supporting that organization. The Giving Circles Fund simply equips young people to be thoughtful with their giving while also making it fun.

PLEDGE 1% (WWW.PLEDGE1PERCENT.ORG)

Pledge 1% is a corporate philanthropy movement dedicated to making the community a key stakeholder in every business. The organization encourages and challenges individuals and companies to pledge 1 percent of equity, product, and employee time for their communities. This is known as the "1/1/1 model."

Pledge 1% founding partners include Atlassian, Entrepreneurs Foundation of Colorado, and Salesforce Foundation. In

2014, they came together to accelerate their shared vision that every business around the globe should integrate philanthropy into its corporate DNA.

Each founding organization embraced corporate philanthropy early on and was interested in helping and encouraging companies around the world to integrate the 1/1/1 model easily from the beginning. Pledge 1% was launched on Giving Tuesday in 2014 to help more companies create and build the 1/1/1 model into their business plans.

The goal for Pledge 1% is to inspire and activate early-stage philanthropy in corporations. By committing just 1 percent of a company's equity, time, and product from the beginning, companies can ensure a greater impact in the future. Taking the pledge is intended to be simple. The first step in the process is to make a pledge on the Pledge 1% website. From there, Pledge 1% works with companies to help set the strategy for their giving programs and to connect them with relevant resources.

According to Dipti Pratt, the director of Pledge 1% who runs the organization out of the Entrepreneurs Foundation of Colorado, a variety of companies, from new private enterprises to well-established multinational corporations, have taken a pledge. Different companies want and need different things. Some already have a clear methodology for what they are doing philanthropically, while others might want to define their vision and strategy for giving. A company might need to figure out what's appropriate for its organization and how it can be most impactful by leveraging the resources it already has. Dipti says that Pledge 1% offers services in the form of mentorship, education, and evaluation; they also act as an important sounding board as businesses go through the process of defining their philanthropic vision. In addition to receiving guidance from the Pledge 1% team, companies can connect with like-minded organizations that have made the same pledge and support each other in reaching their corporate responsibility goals to maximize community impact.

There is currently no fee for being part of Pledge 1%. The founding partners are underwriting the work because they want to foster a movement that has real impact. They want to engage with the companies dedicated to integrated corporate philanthropy and, as a result, are taking the barrier of cost for these programs out of the equation. Dipti says that a small donation to the nonprofit organization is asked, but not required, at the end of the work.

In a nutshell, Pledge 1% wants to see companies take a pledge so the organization can recognize the donors for their work and commitment to the community, help formulate how their giving will work, and connect them to the necessary resources. In its first three months, Pledge 1% worked with sixty companies. They would like to reach five hundred by Giving Tuesday 2015. Their goal is for any company anywhere to be able to integrate giving into their corporate structure, to help achieve sustainable social impact and to make our communities more vibrant.

B1G1 GIVING LIFE (WWW.B1G1.COM/GIVINGLIFE)

Giving Life from B1G1 is a unique giving platform that allows you to link life-changing giving projects of your choice to everyday activities. It is designed like an online giving journal. You give and impact lives whenever you do something you enjoy, easily incorporating giving into everyday life.

Once you set up a free account, you start by choosing life activities that you want to link to your giving. You can choose things like dining out, watching or playing sports, driving, caring for a pet, or shopping online. There is also an option to create your own activity. From there, you choose a project you will support each time you do a chosen activity. For example, you might choose to give others access to life-saving water every time you have a coffee. The organization designates how much you should donate each time you perform the given activity. Some projects cost as little as 1¢ per activity to support.

After you determine which activities you will tie to your giving and which projects you will support, you indicate how often you will perform the activity and make the donation. The quantity you choose depends upon your giving period. The website calculates your donation as you enter the numbers. You either donate right away or set a reminder so you remember to go back and make your donation once per week, once per month, or every three, six, or twelve months.

Because the Giving Life platform is set up as an online giving journal, you can easily track and share your giving impact. You can see your giving grow visually from a seed to a fully grown plant as you increase your giving. Giving Life members can also make "giving connections" through the site utilizing their Facebook profiles. There are options to create groups to involve others in your giving and to make "wishes" that show your giving goal and how close you are to achieving it.

B1G1 uses the power of its membership-based Business for Good program to support the Giving Life for individual giving. The B1G1 Business for Good program empowers businesses to allocate a portion of their sales to carefully selected, high-impact projects, adding giving to everyday business activities. Giving for Life users can support the same projects as businesses. There are hundreds of carefully selected projects that are fully vetted by B1G1 to support. As Paul Dunn, chairman of B1G1 shared with me, Giving Life is a great way to start tying activities, whether business related or not, into giving.

EVERYDAYHERO[5] (WWW.EVERYDAYHERO.COM/US)

The website Everydayhero is a global fund-raising platform that allows you to see the impact of your giving. Launched in the United States in April of 2014, the original concept for Everydayhero was developed in 2004 by Simon Lockyer and Nathan Betteridge in Australia. Back then, they started a consumer brand that gave a percentage of its profits to charity. Both had done a lot of work in the nonprofit sector and wanted to incorporate giving into their brand that would sit in big stores.

That product never took off, but they noticed that the Internet was really taking off. They left the stores and went online to create Everydayhero in 2007. Simon tells me that their goal was to make giving easier and more accessible. They saw that nonprofits were poorly funded and that peer-to-peer fund-raising was prevalent.

After a lot of consumer research prior to launching Everydayhero, Simon and Nathan determined that they wanted to go beyond the dollar sign and truly understand what giving means to people. They found that we are motivated when we can see our impact. Showing people the impact of their giving in a quantitative way makes people want to give even more.

Knowing these facts, Simon and his crew set out to measure more than just a dollar amount, to measure also our time, voice, energy, and effort; Everydayhero has integrations with Map-MyFitness, VolunteerMatch, Facebook, and Twitter, allowing users to quantify their own giving footprint.

In 2011, Everydayhero was acquired by the charity software business, Blackbaud, so it is now backed by an established and leading nonprofit technology partner. This allows nonprofit partners, who can join for free, the ability to offer their supporters a simple and powerful way to fund-raise on their behalf.

Users can set up a free account on Everydayhero, create a volunteering goal, and log the hours they have given to their chosen nonprofits. You can also create your own fund-raising pages, which are easily shared and tracked via social media. Runners can track the miles they run for charity. The more you log with Everydayhero, the more you can track. You can see the collective impact you are making with other community members around the world. More than 600,000 people have supported more than 5,000 charities since 2007.

MAKING IT HAPPEN

Gone are the days when you wait to receive an appeal letter, typically timed at the end of the calendar year, to remind you to write a check to a nonprofit. Donating has changed drastically over the years, since people now have access to online tools for researching, advocating for, and donating to worthy nonprofits. Even in a recession, people respond to the pull to give and help others.

As I mentioned earlier, having personal connections to an organization and seeing a tangible and quantifiable impact from my giving makes me want to give more. The stories in this chapter illustrate the different ways in which you can incorporate philanthropy into your everyday life. I have found that donating money is a very personal act. We donate for different reasons. We think it through a bit more because we are giving our hard-earned money and want to make sure it gets put to good use.

Ruth realized that she was still a philanthropist although she felt limited in how much she could give financially, because she was a dedicated, invested board member of a nonprofit close to her heart. The Giving Circles Fund helps future philanthropists become smart givers by offering education and opportunity to participate in giving circles. Pledge 1% is dedicated to helping early-stage companies embrace an integrated philanthropic business model. Both B1G1 Giving Life and Everydayhero offer the power to raise funds and track your impact while doing the things you enjoy most.

A NEW APPROACH TO TRADITIONAL PHILANTHROPY: ACTION STEPS TO GET YOU STARTED

At this point, I hope you feel more confident that you have the ability to be philanthropic, no matter where you are on the income spectrum. The following five suggested action steps will help you get started on your quest to become a philanthropist.

1. *Change Your Definition of Philanthropy*

   If you are reading this book, chances are you are already on your way to redefining the concept of philanthropy. Open your mind to more than just writing a check every now and then. Think about ways in which you can make the most impact with what you have in a way that's sustainable over time.

2. *Identify Who You Can Team Up with and Create a Giving Circle*

   Think about like-minded people you might want to team up with to pool money and create a giving circle. Giving circles are a great way to start the process of researching and identifying the causes you want to support. Working alongside others allows your giving to become more consistent and strategic.

3. *Figure Out What You Are Capable of Giving*

    If you want to challenge yourself, you might start your own personal giving pledge—potentially even giving on a daily basis. You might also consider impact investing. If possible, sit down with an accountant or financial planner to discuss what you are capable of donating. At the very least, calculate what 1 percent of your income looks like each month and go from there. You'd be surprised at the difference between how much you can give versus how much you think you can give.

4. *Find Your Cause (or Causes)*

    Because donating is a personal decision, make sure you know where you want to put your money. You don't have to choose one cause. You can certainly experiment by supporting many causes, as I have. You'll find resources below to help you with your research.

5. *Give!*

    Start making small donations every month to your favorite cause. Fund a microloan. Tie your activities to giving. Join a nonprofit as a board member. Create a giving circle with friends. Whatever you decide to do, the key is to start giving.

You won't know the right way for you to give until you take action!

A NEW APPROACH TO TRADITIONAL PHILANTHROPY: RESOURCES

Philanthropy Research and Education

- Indie Philanthropy Toolkit (www.indiephilanthropy.org /toolkit/resources): Indie Philanthropy is a "creative disruption to the status quo of funding." They have curated some spectacular resources for donor education and share a reading list that includes reports, resources, and articles to keep you "active and inspired."

- Giving Circles Fund Resources (www.givingcirclesfund.org /learn): You've read about the Giving Circles Fund dedication to educating young philanthropists. This page includes a giving circle facilitation guide, a book list, and links to relevant articles, resources, and research on philanthropy.

- Pledge 1% Resources (www.pledge1percent.org/resources .html): Dedicated to educating businesses on the 1/1/1 model, the Pledge 1% resources page includes information about donating 1 percent of equity, time, and product—and resources to help you build your program within your business.

- Find Your Passion Worksheet (www.givingcirclesfund.org
  /static/opf_philcurriculum_findyourpassion-1.pdf): If you
  are having trouble finding a cause to support, this handy
  worksheet is sure to help. Developed by the Giving Circles
  Fund in partnership with the Center for Philanthropy and
  Nonprofit Leadership, it asks questions to help you narrow
  your passions into causes you want to support.

- GuideStar (www.guidestar.org): The GuideStar website
  gives you access to the most complete, up-to-date nonprofit
  data available, helpful when vetting organizations you are
  thinking of donating to.

- GiveWell (www.givewell.org): GiveWell is a nonprofit dedicated to finding "outstanding giving opportunities and
  publishing the full details of [their] analysis to help donors
  decide where to give."

- GreatNonprofits (www.greatnonprofits.org): GreatNonprofits is the largest nonprofit review website available. You can
  search for reviews and ratings of nonprofits or leave your own
  rating and review.

5   Giving Model 3:
Shopping with a Conscience

Think globally, act locally.

How much do you think about the products you are buying? Beyond the obvious fact that you need or want an actual item, have you considered the effect of your purchase? I am guessing most people don't stop and think about every single purchase they make. Who has the time?

We are living in a world that wants to shop more consciously. It was reported in the 2013 Cone Communications Social Impact Survey that 88 percent of Americans would stop buying products if they learned of a company's irresponsible or deceptive business practices.[1] On a global level, the 2013 Cone Communications Global CSR Study reported that if given the opportunity, 92 percent of consumers would buy a product that has a social and/or environmental benefit.[2]

Those statistics sound great, but the same surveys noted the need for more transparency from companies. Businesses can say they have environmentally friendly products or that they donate proceeds of sales to a cause in order to entice us to purchase products—and it seems to be a popular thing to do these days—but to be honest, it's not always easy to shop consciously because many of the biggest companies in the world that we buy from are not as transparent as they should be about their business practices. If consumers knew which companies were making empty promises, they would stop supporting them.

This giving model is one that can seem daunting at first. However, when you know what to look for and make shopping consciously a habit, it does become easier.

So what exactly does it mean to shop with a conscience? There are several factors to consider and questions you might ask yourself while shopping online or in a store, including the following:

- Where was the product made?
- Who made the product?
- Are the workers treated fairly and ethically?
- What kind of carbon footprint is the product leaving behind?
- Is the product safe for the environment?
- Does the company that made the product have ethical business practices?

To be fair, you are not always going to be able to find this information and you might not have the time to do the research. But I would still encourage you to make shopping with a conscience a priority—big-box stores may be convenient, but they are not always the best places to find products made with the highest ethical standards in mind. The problem with big-box stores is that the focus tends to be on the quantity of products offered and keeping prices low. With so many companies and products represented in a store, it is difficult to monitor how each affects people and the environment. I'm not saying everything in a big-box store is bad for you or the environment, but there are other places you might consider shopping first.

Following are some basic rules of thumb for you to use the next time you shop. You can pick one and start from there or simply keep all of them in mind the next time you purchase a product. I am the first to admit that I am not always a conscious shopper. I am getting better at it, and it helps when you know what to look for.

SHOP LOCALLY

When talking about shopping with a conscience, I always recommend going to locally owned stores in the neighborhood. These are the stores that are owned by your neighbors and fellow community members. If you are as lucky as I am, you might even be able to walk or bike to these stores, saving the environment from the additional carbon monoxide pollution from your car.

The Shop Local movement has gained considerable momentum in the past few years. It makes sense, considering the economic downturn that began in 2008 and affected individuals, families, and businesses across the country. Americans have turned their attention more and more to Main Street instead of Wall Street. Supporting local businesses is good for the economy and helps your local community and neighbors. Though it was started by the credit card giant American Express, Small Business Saturday has become a popular campaign that encourages people to get their holiday shopping done in their local neighborhood the day after Black Friday.

The great thing about shopping locally is that you can actually get to know the shopkeepers and learn more about the products they sell and the companies they work with. Shopping small can give you the opportunity to request specific items as well. Often, local stores offer products that can't be found anywhere else in the United States, especially handcrafted items made with local materials. Who wouldn't want a unique gift or souvenir from a neighborhood store?

LOOK FOR FAIR TRADE PRODUCTS

Fair trade, in its simplest form, is a movement to provide fair prices to producers of goods in developing countries, with the goal of reducing poverty, treating workers in an ethical way, and promoting environmentally sustainable practices.

You've probably seen fair trade coffee in your local grocery store or coffee shop. When you purchase that coffee, you know that the farmers who produced the coffee beans—most likely in a remote part of a developing country—received a fair price for their crop. They are connected to importers, providing them with long-term sustainability, and are guaranteed a minimum price for their coffee.

Fair trade goes beyond providing jobs and humane working conditions. As the Fair Trade Federation notes on its website, "communities are improved; nutritional needs met; health care costs are covered; the poor, especially women, are empowered; the environmental impact of production, sourcing, and transport is mitigated to the fullest extent possible." All of the clothing from the fair trade company INDIGE-NOUS, for example, is artisan hand-made, comes from fair trade artisan cooperatives, and uses organic fibers and environmentally friendly dyes. They include a "trace tool" on the hang tag that tells you about the artisan who made the garment. You can even hear the creator tell her own story via video when you scan a QR code with your smartphone.

Purchasing fair trade products can actually change the lives of an entire family. By buying fair trade, we support businesses that provide education for children and offer jobs to women who might otherwise become victims of sex trafficking. If an item is marked as fair trade, you also know that it has met strict guidelines in order to be certified.

FIND PRODUCTS THAT GIVE BACK

Shopping for products that give back in some way through your purchase is an alternative to buying fair trade products. Because of the arduous, and sometimes expensive, process involved in becoming fair trade certified, some companies use the same basic principles or build a giving component directly into their products.

Shopping fair trade is just one of many options available to socially conscious consumers. Gifts that give back often become popular during the holiday season or during months dedicated to raising awareness for certain causes, such as breast cancer awareness month in October, but you can find products that give back year round.

Up to 50 percent of profits made from sales of (RED) products go to fight AIDS in Africa. Organizations like Save the Children and Heifer International give you the option to adopt or purchase animals for families in developing nations so they can generate income. UncommonGoods supports talented artisans all around the world while also donating to a chosen charity on behalf of the buyer. You can even find lingerie that gives back. Empowered By You is a luxury lingerie brand created by the Seven Bar Foundation, a nonprofit organization that uses microfinance to empower women around the globe.

You may be familiar with the business model of One for One or "buy one, give one," made popular by TOMS, who started out by giving one pair of shoes to a child in need for every pair sold. You'll find this model used by Naked Specs, a prescription eyeglass company based in Perth, Australia. For every purchase made, they donate five pairs of glasses or funds of equivalent value to provide eye treatment, such as cataract surgery, for people in developing countries. Po Campo sells unique weatherproof bags made with vegan fabrics designed for an active, urban lifestyle. For every twenty-five bags Po Campo sells through its online store, a schoolgirl in Africa will get a new bicycle. Even big-box stores like Macy's offer socially conscious brands such as Heart of Haiti, which provides sustainable income for a Haitian artisan and her extended family.

These are just a few examples of products you can feel good about purchasing. You can find a continually updated list of gifts that give back at simplegivinglab.com/gifts-that-give -back.

CONSIDER THE ENVIRONMENTAL IMPACT

Let's face it—not all of the products we need are going to be readily available from a fair trade company or one that is locally owned or donates proceeds to charity. Everyday items like toiletries, clothes, and food are most often bought out of convenience and necessity. We don't always have the time to stop and think about each and every item we buy.

I remember sitting in a graduate-level organizational leadership class discussing the intricacies of how our products actually end up in our hands. Have you ever stopped to think about the environment in which the products you buy were made or how they got to you? There are so many steps in the process, from manufacturing that product to packaging and shipping it. Do you know where those products are made? What kinds of materials are used? What natural resources may be affected? How ethical the company's business practices are?

Whether we like it or not, sometimes the products made

by gigantic companies and sold at big-box stores are the most convenient option, especially at the last minute. If you want to truly shop consciously, you can take the time to do some research on the products and companies from which you typically purchase. You can do this by researching the countries in which the products are made. Some countries are notorious for their treatment of factory workers and the environment. Look on tags and packaging. If a company doesn't disclose where the products are made, take a moment to contact the company and ask.

Another way to research the products and companies you buy from is to look up their corporate social responsibility (CSR) programs online. If one doesn't exist or is extremely hard to find, that is your first red flag. CSR policies should state a company's stance on what has been termed the "triple bottom line" of people, planet, and profit. While a company's CSR program is largely self-regulated, it can tell you how dedicated the company is to being responsible and accountable for social and environmental issues. Those that embrace CSR in their business model will go above and beyond treating workers decently and minimizing their carbon footprint.

To put these shopping guidelines into practice, let's take a look at a few companies and websites that are making it easier for everyday consumers to shop with a conscience.

NEARBY REGISTRY (WWW.NEARBYREGISTRY.COM)

Nearby Registry is a website that allows you to shop and register for unique gifts from local shops and nonprofits. The website acts as a marketplace for anyone who wants to support local businesses, whether they are down the street or across the country.

The idea for NEARBY came about in 2009 when Allison Grappone got engaged and her family and friends kept asking what she and her fiancé wanted for gifts. Not wanting to sign up for a traditional registry at the big-box stores, she created a simple Google Doc that listed the things they wanted and needed. Some of the items were traditional wedding requests, while others were not. Armed with an MBA and work experience in sustainable business, economic development, and renewable energy, Allison started to research ways in which she could shift the type of gifts we give and reduce our consumption.

Allison noted that the gift registry business was a $19 billion industry that local businesses did not have a piece of. For several years, she worked on her idea for a traditional registry that could incorporate local, independent businesses. In 2011, she won $25,000 from the Manchester Young Professionals Network in New Hampshire to fund the project and was able to put together a team that would help her make Nearby Registry a reality.

When you visit the NEARBY website, you'll find a variety of gifts, from cookware and table linens to artwork and baby clothes. You can even make charitable donations to support local nonprofits. You can shop for gifts or for yourself and purchase universal gift cards.

Anyone can create a registry on NEARBY, and Allison notes that people can decide what is "local" to them. Her team will work with registrants to add the products they want from their area, or they can simply choose what is already available on the website knowing that each company on NEARBY is a confirmed independently owned and operated business and does not pay any royalties to franchise companies.

Allison and her team also work to make sure it's easy for businesses to join and take advantage of the selling platform that NEARBY offers. The independent businesses you find on NEARBY pay a one-time setup fee, connect to a payment processor, and pay a transaction fee when sales are made.

Allison launched NEARBY in her home state of New Hampshire, but she is looking to expand the website nationally. She has worked with businesses in Seattle, Portland (Maine *and* Oregon), and Burlington, Vermont, and is seeking partnerships with local business groups. Of course, anyone can order the products on NEARBY, no matter the location. Allison estimates that approximately $3,000 to $6,000 is kept in local economies through a NEARBY gift registry.

Even if you aren't looking to start a registry or shop for a gift, NEARBY offers a simple and easy way to keep money in local businesses and nonprofits around the United States.

ARTISAN BUSINESS NETWORK

(WWW.ARTISANBUSINESSNETWORK.COM)

Artisan Business Network (ABN) was developed by Fairwinds Trading and the HAND/EYE Fund in 2011 with a mission to empower the artisan culture of Haiti and improve community well-being.

The combination of the trade embargos of the 1990s, political instability, and the devastating earthquake in January 2010 shrank Haiti's exports of handmade goods considerably. Willa Shalit, CEO of Fairwinds Trading, was able to bring Haitian products to Macy's after the crippling earthquake. She showed the department store that it was not donations that the country needed, but support for the artisans whose traditional handicrafts could lessen the country's dependency on foreign aid. Seeing the rich artist community firsthand, Macy's was eager to bring the products of these Haitian craftspeople to market. Macy's launched the Heart of Haiti product line for sale online and in stores around the United States.

When Nathalie Tancrede, a Haitian-American living in New York City, saw what Willa was doing for her struggling home country, she reached out to see if she could help. Willa brought Nathalie on as a volunteer translator, and after their first night in Haiti, offered her a job as the director of Heart of Haiti. What Nathalie thought would be a three- to six-month commitment has turned into four years and counting. Though she left a very good life and her family in New York, Nathalie understood the importance of her work in Haiti. She learned very quickly that though Haitians may not have a lot, they are still happy and resilient people.

While Macy's still offers the Heart of Haiti collection, Nathalie has helped to grow the organization into what is now the ABN, which has found even more clients for Haitian artists. With a staff of twelve, the ABN connects the artists with global markets. Nathalie tells me that they go out and look for existing groups of artisans who are interested in training. The ABN works with artisans to give them the tools and training they need in areas ranging from product development to financial literacy so they can become successful entrepreneurs.

They focus on preserving traditional approaches to Haitian art while also meeting product demand. Creators learn about market trends and the channels in which their products will have to travel, so they can create the highest quality goods, taking things like materials and packaging into consideration. They learn how to develop collections to meet market demand for a more sustainable business.

To further encourage its members to understand and grow their businesses, the ABN also brings artisans to the New York Now gift show. There, the craftspeople are able to experience a trade show, meet clients, see other products being offered, and then share what they've learned with their peers when they go back home. Nathalie says this real-life experience is often better than the ABN teaching in a class.

Using this Trade-Not-Aid approach, Macy's and other ABN partners have paved the way in helping to rebuild an important sector of a fragile economy. There is a fee to become a member of the ABN, which allows access to all of the ABN's services. Though most of the artisans in the network are male, Nathalie and her team are working on reaching out to more female artists.

The ABN currently works with about a thousand artisans who create using a variety of materials, such as metals, papier-mâché, horn and bone, beads, and fabric. The orders these craftspeople receive through clients of the ABN have helped them build homes and get out of the tents that many were living in after the earthquake. Being able to run their own businesses has allowed the artisans to send their children to school, and they are now able to afford better healthcare. You can often read the stories behind the artisans right on the tags when you find products in stores such as Macy's. After four years, Nathalie can already see the impact the ABN has made on the artisans' lives and Haiti's economy. She invites anyone who visits Haiti to come to the local store in Port-au-Prince.

TO THE MARKET (WWW.TOTHEMARKET.COM)

Launched in 2014, TO THE MARKET is an online marketplace that showcases handmade goods created by survivors of abuse, conflict, and disease.

Before starting TO THE MARKET, Jane Mosbacher Morris served as the Director of Humanitarian Action for the McCain Institute and worked in the U.S. Department of State's Bureau of Counterterrorism and the Secretary's Office of Global Women's Issues. Jane has been most interested in people's working conditions. She believes that even social issues are market driven and that providing economic independence to others can break the cycle of poverty.

As a social enterprise, TO THE MARKET takes a three-pronged approach in its business model. They first promote survivor-made goods for purchase through their online marketplace, pop-up shops, custom sourcing, and retail partnerships. In addition, TO THE MARKET shares the inspiring stories of survivors by creating platforms, including its own "Stories" blog and a *Huffington Post* blog, for the survivors and their champions. Finally, TO THE MARKET provides tailored services—including addressing workers' mental health and delivering trend forecasts—to its partners that employ survivors in order to help them improve their production and organizational management.

Jane works with as many partners as possible. She first started with a handful of organizations that she knew worked with survivors—the initial vetting process was already complete because she'd worked with each of them before.

When Jane and her team create new partnerships, they make sure the companies adhere to TO THE MARKET's guiding principles, which include prohibition of child labor, the maintenance of a safe and hospitable workplace environment, fair hours and wages, good corporate citizenship that protects workers' dignity and human rights, and the opportunity for employees to form a labor union or express grievances.

Visitors to the TO THE MARKET website can shop by cause, country, partner, or type of product they are looking for. You can find beautifully handmade clothes, shoes, bags, home goods, jewelry, and accessories.

Jane says that the survivors employed by TO THE MARKET partners are not only given an opportunity to achieve economic independence but they are also changing their children's trajectory, as many were at risk of being exploited.

CLIMATE MAMA (WWW.CLIMATEMAMA.COM)

Harriet Shugarman had worked in and around climate issues at the United Nations for several years when the initial U.N. Earth Summit was held in 1992. It was the first time climate was being discussed at that level, and many commissions, including the Commission on Sustainable Development, were set up as a result. Still, Harriet wondered how and if these global conferences were making a difference.

Harriet's fast-paced career as a policy analyst and economist slowed down once she had her two children. After the events of 9/11, her family moved from New York City to the suburbs. While she admits to not realizing how serious the climate crisis was at the time, she could see that the issue was not resonating with the parents around her.

Everything changed when Harriet had the unique opportunity to be one of the first thousand people to participate in a training with former vice president Al Gore. Sponsored by the Climate Reality Project, the goal of that training was to educate the public on climate change. She realized then that climate change was a very real and current problem. Harriet started to think of ways to reach those parents who weren't aware of the seriousness of the situation.

Climate Mama was launched in 2010 with the original intention of testing products to see how environmentally friendly they were. Harriet could see that bloggers were reaching parents in a strong, peer-to-peer manner and started to blog about the climate issues she couldn't find being discussed elsewhere. What evolved was a robust website that explains what climate change is, gives tips to parents on how to talk to their kids about it, and offers environmentally friendly product suggestions to help reduce our carbon footprint.

As Climate Mama has evolved, a strong advocacy arm has also developed. Harriet notes that there are so many things that parents can do on a local level, from speaking up against ordinances that may limit the use of solar panels to opting for snack foods that are made by companies who follow sustainable practices. Climate Mama encourages people to look beyond signing petitions by talking to legislators and gives them the resources to do so.

Harriet embraces the role of climate change educator and spokesperson for parents. She wants to be in front of legislators talking about how we need to move forward on renewable energy. Instead of looking at climate change as a big, scary problem that is impossible to tackle, she wants to embrace it as an opportunity to focus on positive solutions. She looks to the success of Mothers Against Drunk Driving (MADD) as an example of parents coming together as a political force to make a difference.

While climate change can be a complex topic to explain, Climate Mama first encourages people to start educating themselves through articles on its blog. From there, Harriet urges readers to find like-minded people or groups in their local area who also want to make a difference, because it's easier to make an impact when you are part of a team. Taking that first step will help you make your second step. You might start with small changes, like purchasing orange juice from a company that has environmentally friendly business practices and talking to your children about it. Everything balloons from that first step.

Climate Mama also wants people to consider climate when voting for elected officials.

When it comes to climate, the more we talk about it—with our kids, neighbors, friends, and legislators—the more we can do to protect it.

CLIMATE COUNTS[3] (WWW.CLIMATECOUNTS.ORG)

As mentioned previously in this chapter, making purchase decisions based on the carbon footprint of the product's maker can be a daunting task. It's great to consider, but not so easy to practice.

Much of what we buy, from toilet paper to clothes, is made by some of the largest companies in the world. These companies are big enough to make a strong impact—positive and negative—on our planet. But who holds them accountable?

Gary Hirshberg, chairman and former CEO of Stonyfield Farm, an organic yogurt producer in New Hampshire, sought to answer this question of accountability. He saw how economic boycotts in South Africa eventually ended apartheid. He thought, why not develop a scorecard that shows how companies are doing with their carbon footprint?

Climate Counts was born from the idea that holding companies accountable for their influence on climate change will lead to more sustainable business practices. The nonprofit organization brings consumers and companies together in the fight against global climate change. As Climate Counts project director Mike Bellamente told me, they score consumer-relevant companies in sixteen readily identifiable sectors ranging from airlines to pharmaceuticals. Companies are scored on a 0–100 scale based on twenty-two questions over four criteria to determine if they have

- MEASURED their climate "footprint,"
- REDUCED their impact on global warming,
- SUPPORTED progressive climate legislation,
- Publicly DISCLOSED their climate actions clearly and comprehensively.

Climate Counts also give consumers the opportunity to raise their voice against those companies who might not be up to par. You can e-mail companies directly, via the Climate Counts website, to let them know you are watching them and that their scores matter to you. There's an app you can download on your smartphone so you can look up scores and voice your views on the go.

In addition, Climate Counts provides sustainability consulting through their Industry Innovators program.

Mike noted in our conversation that the scorecard does have its flaws. It doesn't take into account how workers are treated, for example, and it is hard to translate the scoring when applied to specific brands within a company. But it is a start. Climate Counts is ahead of its time with regards to measurement and the scorecard makes this type of information more accessible to the public; the simple tool helps to keep companies accountable.

MAKING IT HAPPEN

The purpose of this chapter is to show you how easy it can be to shop with a conscience. I am the first to admit that adhering to all of these guidelines on conscious shopping on a regular basis is not easy. Sometimes we just need to run out and grab something from the store or quickly order a gift online. However, if we become more mindful of our actions when we make purchases and stop to think about where the products come from, we can make a difference. We can make it a point to shop locally, choose fair trade products, look for gifts that give back, and consider the carbon footprint of our purchase. Even Amazon, the largest Internet-based company in the United States, allows you to support your favorite charitable organization through AmazonSmile, at no cost to you, every time you shop. There are also monthly subscription services you can join, such as Love with Food and Conscious Box, that allow you to sample natural foods and ethical products every month while also giving back. The trick is to know these options exist.

NEARBY Registry gives you the opportunity to register for unique gifts and to support local businesses that may not even be local to you. When you buy products made by members of the Artisan Business Network, you know you are supporting the rebuilding of a developing nation. Websites like TO THE MARKET offer an array of goods that also give back by supporting the survivors that make the products. Climate Mama and Climate Counts help educate you on the effects your purchases have on the environment and give you the opportunity to be a better consumer advocate.

SHOPPING WITH A CONSCIENCE: ACTION STEPS TO GET YOU STARTED

Now that you know how to shop more consciously, it's time to get into action mode. Below are some action steps and resources to help you get shopping with a conscience.

1. *Change Your Mind-set When You Shop*

   The first step is to make it a point to be more observant about where you shop and what you buy. It may take a little legwork, but you can do this. And you don't need to break the bank to replace products that just aren't cutting it. Look at what is available to you, create your plan, and start implementing small changes.

2. *Plan Your Conversion*

   It can be overwhelming to think about making many changes all at once. For example, you do not have to throw out everything in your cupboard of cleaning supplies if you are concerned about environmental effects. Rather, as you run out of a product, replace it with a more eco-friendly version. Do some background research on the products you find in your closet and in your home. Make it a point to look for local options when shopping. Choose fair trade coffee over regular coffee. Step by step these small decisions will become more of a habit over time.

3. *Choose a Cause*

   Shopping with a conscience can mean different things to different people. In your plan, it might be helpful to determine whether your cause is environmental, a focus on social good, or something else. Having a passion for what you are supporting can make you feel even better about your purchase.

You might decide to start focusing on finding products that support your local economy before you start looking at purchasing gifts with a more global focus. There is no right or wrong approach.

4. *Share Your Passion with Others*

   When giving a gift that supports your cause, be sure to explain to the recipient why this particular gift is so special. Tell them how the gift affects people and communities locally and globally. Encourage your friends and family to shop consciously as well. Teach them how to make better purchasing decisions and share your tools and resources with them.

5. *Raise Your Children to Shop with a Conscience*

   We learn how to shop from our parents, caregivers, and adult role models. Talking to kids about the products we buy, how they are made, and the effect our purchases have on people and the environment can be powerful. Teaching our kids how to be mindful about shopping at a young age will make for conscious shoppers in the future. Be sure to include your kids in your conscious shopping excursions and ask them for their own ideas to shop with a conscience!

SHOPPING WITH A CONSCIENCE: RESOURCES

Shopping Local

- U.S. Chamber of Commerce Directory (www.uschamber
  .com/chamber/directory): If you aren't familiar with the
  local businesses available to you in your community, searching your local Chamber of Commerce can be a great place
  to start.

- Yahoo! Local (local.yahoo.com): Since not every business is
  going to be a member of your local chamber, you might also
  turn to the Yahoo! Local listings in your area where you
  will find local businesses, restaurants, and services along
  with reviews.

- American Express Shop Small Map (shopsmallnow.ameri
  canexpress.com/ShopSmall): American Express offers a map
  of small businesses around the country that is searchable
  by various categories, including shopping, services, dining,
  travel, and entertainment. If you are a cardholder, you can
  also log in and get recommendations based on your spending history.

- Downtown Associations: A basic Google search of the downtown associations in your area can give you access to a list of

businesses that are active in the community. These associations often bring together local shops and restaurants to offer events and special discounts during the holidays.

Fair Trade Products

- Fair for all Shopping Guide (www.fairforallguide.com): With the goal of supporting the rights of everyone making the products we buy, this website and blog is a tool to make it easier for you to find ethically made products.
- Fair Trade USA (www.fairtradeusa.org/products-partners): The Fair Trade USA website allows you to search for Fair Trade Certified products and partners and has information on fair trade business practices and how to become certified.
- Fair Trade Federation (www.fairtradefederation.org): The Fair Trade Federation website includes information on fair trade and building a fair trade business. You can also search for fair trade wholesale suppliers, stores, cafés, products, and members.
- Shop with a Conscience Consumer Guide (www.sweatfree .org/shopping): A guide from SweatFree Communities and International Labor Rights Forum that includes products made in good working conditions by people organized into democratic unions or worker-owned cooperatives.

- Better World Shopper (www.betterworldshopper.org): According to the website, Better World Shopper is dedicated to providing people with a comprehensive, up-to-date, and reliable account of every company on the planet's commitment to social and environmental responsibility and making it available in practical forms that individuals can use in their everyday lives.

- Free 2 Work (www.free2work.org): A website and mobile app that can help you learn about how your favorite brands are working to address forced and child labor. The goal is to shed light on the many hands that products go through in order to get to us.

Gifts That Give Back

- There are many options out there for products with a purpose and gifts that give back, several of which are mentioned in this book. I maintain a list of products, stores, and resources at simplegivinglab.com/giftsthatgiveback.

Ethical/Eco-Friendly Shopping and Resources

- The ClimateStore (www.climatestore.com/shop) is an incredibly valuable resource dedicated to providing products and ideas that will reduce your carbon footprint and lead to lower carbon living.

- Ethical Barcode (www.ethicalbarcode.com) is a free mobile app that helps you make informed decisions at the grocery store by providing information about companies' values on child labor, animal testing, deforestation, and other ethical issues.

- GoodGuide (www.goodguide.com): Scientists rate products on a 0–10 scale for their social, environmental, and health impact. Reviews and ratings are available online and via a mobile app.

- Wikirate.org (www.wikirate.org) provides collaboratively edited content to promote corporate transparency. You can browse by company or by fifteen social and environmental topics.

- Climate Mama (www.climatemama.com): As mentioned earlier in this chapter, Climate Mama helps you get the facts to understand climate change and global warming and act on reducing your carbon footprint.

- Climate Counts (www.climatecounts.org): Also featured in this chapter, Climate Counts scores the world's largest companies on their environmental impact, spurring corporate environmental responsibility and conscious consumption. You can find the scorecards online and via the mobile app.

6 Giving Model 4:
Taking Action on Your Passion

*There are just moments in your life when
your calling comes to you. When you just
know—finally—what you're supposed
to do with your life.*

Alysia Butler, SenseAbility Gym

At some point in your life, you may find that the pull to give is stronger than normal. A simple act of kindness, donating money, or supporting good causes through indirect actions isn't enough. You might be directly affected by a disease that no one knows about or you might observe an action that you just can't sit back and watch. You want to act. You want to educate. You want to change people's minds and perceptions. But how?

Many people don't know how to take action regarding the issues that they are passionate about. I am still working on this piece of my overall giving strategy. Writing about giving to inspire others is one specific actionable item I have been working on, from blogging to authoring this book. I didn't know where to start, so I looked for inspiration from others. I found I was overthinking my intentions. I thought I had to do more when I really just needed to sit down and write.

What's holding us back? Is it fear? The thought of doing what you love, what you are most passionate about, is both exciting and scary. Exciting because you'd be working on that thing that moves you. Scary because, what if it doesn't work? Many people don't move to the point of action because they simply don't think they can make a difference—enacting change can be an incredibly daunting task. Typically, those who take action on their passion have identified something that is not currently being done. Doubt seeps in fast, and it's often hard for even your closest friends, family, and colleagues to understand what you are trying to do.

There are examples all around us of how people take their passion and use it to promote social good. We just have to look. Sometimes, when you start, you may not even consider yourself a philanthropist. You just want to right a wrong or spread a message that people aren't receiving. You have something to say and you need a vehicle with which to say it. There's that something that you really love doing, and you want to take it to the next level. That something that keeps you up at night and won't let you rest until you do something about it.

If you recall, the first two components to meaningful giving are being passionate about a specific cause and acting in a way that benefits someone or something else. Ask yourself, what am I passionate about? What makes you want to jump out of your chair and yell? What makes you happiest? What pushes you over the deep end? Everyone is passionate about something, whether it is animals, the environment, children, or cars. The passion can be anything that moves you.

If you already have a passion, you are halfway there. Sometimes, it's not so obvious how to take that passion into the action stage. In fact, sometimes you might fall into a giving situation without realizing it. Think about what you can do with your passion that will benefit others.

Taking action is easier than you think. You just have to take the time to examine your passion and figure out how it fits in your life. Then, you can work on coming up with a giving model that works for you. For a sustainable giving model, the key is to make that action a regular part of your life or business.

Let's look at the stories of five people who acted on their passions, and as a result, helped support people, animals, and neighborhoods. These are everyday people who, with little or no capital, started businesses and projects simply to help others.

THE JITEGEMEE PROJECT[1]

(WWW.JITEGEMEE PROJECT.ORG)

After finishing her master's degree in education at Stanford University, Adele Miller felt the need to give back to the developing world. She and her sister taught in East Africa in the late 1960s, shortly after Tanzania had gained its independence and started to allow girls into the classroom.

Forty years later, some of the students they taught had become qualified and experienced teachers. Adele and her sister developed a strong bond with these women over the years and shared a vision of creating a primary school complex.

The Jitegemee Project was born when Adele and her sister realized that not much had changed since they had taught in Tanzania decades before. While women and girls were more common in the classroom, the schools had just as many needs.

Jitegemee is a Swahili word that signifies the energy, spirit, and commitment that one individual or a community has deep within that brings about growth in themselves and others. "Education is the key to life" is the Jitegemee Project's motto. Their specific goal is to contribute to the much-needed education facilities in Tanzania by building a fully equipped primary school complex in Buyuni, a newly developing residential area outside the capital of Tanzania.

There are seven phases to the Jitegemee Project, from the initial buying of the land to the completion of the interior finishings. All of the workers are locally hired, and two Catholic Tanzanian Sisters provide guidance on the development of the project on-site. The complex is coming together piece by piece, and classes are added gradually. While the complex is still under construction, classrooms are also used to house teachers and students. As of January 2015, a second floor has been built. Next on the agenda, once the money is raised, is the roof and glass for the windows. As money comes in, construction continues.

The Jitegemee Project has truly been a global grassroots project, with Adele, in the United States, and her sister and a group of trustees, in England, having led the way. They've held various fund-raising events and worked to spread the word about their project however they can. They've never been paid for their efforts, and they've done the work on their own time. Though Adele's sister passed away in 2012, the group she had formed in the UK is still raising money toward the completion of the Jitegemee School.

When the project is complete, the school will educate more than five hundred students every day. And those students will be taught by hardworking women who are committed to a lifetime of social service just like Adele and her sister.

SENSEABILITY GYM (WWW.SENSEABILITYGYM.COM)[2]
Alysia Butler had a calling. It came to her one spring day. She
knew that with a fellow autism mom, Tina Perriello, she was
supposed to open a nonprofit, parent-led sensory gym for
special-needs kids just like hers.

Alysia is a stay-at-home mom with three boys. Her whole
world changed in December 2009 when her middle son was
diagnosed on the autism spectrum at age three and a half. He
enrolled in the public preschool in their autism program and
started occupational therapy services, in addition to having
one-on-one support in the classroom. Alysia and her family
started learning terms like *sensory integration* and *ABA therapy*
and *social speech*. As her son learned how to interact with the
world around him, the family learned, too. Two years later,
their youngest son would also be diagnosed on the autism
spectrum.

It was at that preschool that Alysia met a supportive group
of autism moms, including Tina. These women taught Alysia
about being a mother and an advocate for her kids and kids
like hers—there was a need in their community that they had
to fill.

Alysia and Tina started to plan the opening of SenseAbility Gym—"a sensory gym for sensational kids." They visited two open sensory gyms sponsored by their local autism alliance. These gyms had occupational therapy equipment specific to the needs of special-needs children that was similar to the equipment their kids used in their school therapy programs. At these gyms, they observed that their kids were happy, and so were the other kids in the room. Most important, they felt the acceptance and support in the room. Alysia noted, "We knew we had to open something like that all year round in our town. And we knew we had to open it as a nonprofit." The only similar gym in her area was run by the public school system and was open only when school was in session.

SenseAbility Gym gives children with special needs a safe, fun indoor area where they can play and accommodate their sensory needs. Kids can swing, jump, and play on the same type of therapeutic equipment and toys used by schools and occupational therapy clinics. Located in Hopedale, the gym is the first of its kind in the Metrowest region of Massachusetts. Knowing that they did not need to start completely from scratch, they modeled their gym after an incredibly successful sensory gym in Brooklyn, New York.

Alysia and Tina believe that all children deserve access to therapeutic equipment. They also know that parents need to interact with their children to figure out what helps them "feel better" and have fun. Alysia and Tina see the gym as a place to accommodate the sensory needs of kids like theirs and to build their kids' social skills by giving them the space to interact with other children like themselves. They see the gym as a place where parents of kids with autism can also interact with moms and dads just like them, creating a valuable support network.

Since SenseAbility Gym opened in February 2013, it has welcomed 480 different families through its doors. Most have come to the sensory gym open playtime, but others also come to social skills/sensory classes, birthday parties, and Mom group outings. The latest social skills group for children with limited verbal skills was offered for free, thanks to a grant from the Flutie Foundation, an organization committed to improving quality of life for people and families living with autism.

THE EVOLVED DOG (www.theevolveddog.com)

The Evolved Dog is an online store that sells canine supplies with a conscience. Launched by Leah Twitchell in August 2013, The Evolved Dog is intended to provide people with a place where they can experience stress-free shopping for their dogs—a place where people who love dogs as much as she does don't have to worry about ingredients, safety, quality, or whether the products are environmentally friendly and cruelty-free.

In Leah's words, "I wanted them to be able to find the highest quality products that would enrich the health and well-being of their animals while supporting domestic producers and helping protect the environment."

Leah initially wanted to open up her own physical store in Brunswick, Maine, where she lived. She was driving more than 25 miles to Portland every time she wanted to buy raw dog food and supplies—and she wished there were higher quality and healthier products available in her own area. It was her father who encouraged her to open an online store in order to offer these products to more people and to avoid the high costs of maintaining a bricks-and-mortar store. In order to follow her passion, Leah took a local class for women entrepreneurs who were just starting out.

Leah's mission with The Evolved Dog is to keep everyone's dogs healthy and happy while making it easy for humans to be conscious shoppers. She wants to be a resource for other dog lovers, educating them on the best products for their canines. She is also an advocate for Natural Dog Training, which focuses on establishing emotional rapport with your dog and recognizes the dog's nature as a group hunter.

According to Leah, her overall focus is on the health of the dogs, being environmentally conscious in her company's business practices, and selling products that are domestically produced, primarily in Maine. She offers soy-, wheat-, and corn-free dog treats and sells dog toys that are recycled or recyclable. Leah also uses recyclable packaging when shipping products to customers. The Evolved Dog tries to source products from microentrepreneurs with similar values. Keeping items organic, local, and cruelty-free is important to Leah, and she strives to transition The Evolved Dog to a 100 percent fair trade policy.

She personally tests all the products with her own dogs, Eva the Diva (a pit bull mix) and Sophie (a boxador), and writes about her experiences on her blog. She uses The Evolved Dog to promote awareness of issues concerning homeless animals, always encouraging adoption and fostering, and welcomes any opportunity to help break the stereotypes about rescues and pit bulls.

In addition to volunteering at her local animal shelter, Leah also donates 5 percent of every purchase to the Kennebec Valley Humane Society so her customers can "feel good about shopping for a cause, supporting an ethical retailer, and getting the very best quality products to enrich the life of their dog."

MOLLY BEARS[3] (WWW.MOLLYBEARS.COM)

Molly Bears makes weighted teddy bears for families who have experienced any form of infant loss, free of charge. Along with sister-in-law and cofounder Amanda Crews, Bridget Crews and her husband, Chris, started Molly Bears after losing their little girl, Molly, just three months prior.

Before Molly died from a tight true knot in her cord, infant loss was not a part of the family history. Bridget had already had three children, in addition to giving birth to a surrogate baby. When she was told, "I'm so sorry, but there is no heartbeat," her world crumbled. Bridget then saw life for what it had always been—delicate and fragile.

Bridget needed to do something. She needed to make herself feel better and less helpless. On June 28, 2010, she, her husband, children, and Amanda created what would be the very first "Molly Bear." The bear was weighted so it felt just like holding their infant daughter. Bridget was able to breathe while holding this Molly Bear. Bridget explains that she knew in her heart that "our Molly was gently pushing us. She had been here for a purpose. She wanted us to help others."

Two weeks after creating the first Molly Bear, Bridget started asking other ladies from a stillbirth support group if they would like her to make them bears. With the encouragement of her husband, Bridget created and sent out five bears in that first month. Making those bears helped Bridget and her family through their grief because they felt like they were doing something to help others who were in a similar situation.

By August 2010, Bridget and Amanda created a plan, started buying supplies, and obtained a business license. With a small investment of their own money and some donations from friends and family, they officially started Molly Bears.

In just four and a half years, Molly Bears grew to include twenty bear makers located all over the United States. These volunteer bear makers create two hundred to three hundred bears every month, which are sent to all fifty American states and twenty-eight other countries. Molly Bears can also be found in four hospitals. Many of the bear makers work in memory of an infant that they lost in their own family.

HOPE PRODUCTS INTERNATIONAL
(WWW.HOPE-PRODUCTS.COM)

Hope Products International is a business-as-mission company that is committed to reducing poverty and injustice around the world through product partnerships that advance and improve the lives of women and men.

Launched in October 2014, Hope Products International came about when Lori MacMath and her husband, Scott, decided that they wanted to do more to support the fair trade business that their good friends had started in India. Daughters of Hope is a faith-based organization that takes marginalized women out of bad situations such as sex trafficking and trains them to run their own textile businesses. This organization that their friends started also provides these women with meals and child care.

One night, Lori, Scott, and another couple had a conversation about how Daughters of Hope had only one distributor in the United States. They wondered what it would be like if they could support ministries and businesses like Daughters of Hope as well as missionaries on the ground. Inspired by that late-night conversation, they began their year-long process of getting a business started.

As Lori put it, "We are at halftime in life. Are we going to sit and be comfortable or are we going to do something?"

They decided to do something.

Hope Products International empowers missionaries and oppressed women and men around the world by selling their products and telling their stories. The process begins when missionaries develop relationships with marginalized men and women, listening to their stories, sharing information about their faith, and offering them work that pays a fair wage. Hope Products International then sells the products through an online store, independent sales agents, and fund-raisers at American churches and schools.

Hope Products International designs and sells textile products made by the Daughters of Hope in Bangalore, including bags, scarves, lanyards, and key chains made from upcycled saris and burlap that has been discarded. They have also partnered with a Chinese company that produces drinkware and canvases. Although China is known as a place that cheaply produces and exports items to America, Hope Products International has partnered with a manufacturer that offers fair wages and safe working conditions and whose factory is run by a Christian woman.

Hope Products International is looking to continue to replicate the model they are using in India and China by partnering with other missionaries. They hope to eventually open a warehouse in the United States that employs people in their own backyard, and they are particularly interested in partnering with other businesses that work with human trafficking survivors to make and sell products. Lori says they want to be a compassionate company that gives employees something sustainable—work, community, child care, life skills, and more.

MAKING IT HAPPEN

In every example discussed in this chapter, the women and men that started organizations with a humanitarian mission in mind relied on the support of their community. The Jitegemee Project, SenseAbility Gym, and Molly Bears are registered 501(c) (3) nonprofit organizations. They have boards of directors to keep them accountable, and they depend on donations and grants to keep them running. Not one of the founders is doing the work for the money. They put countless hours into their causes, and they see results because they have friends, family, volunteers, and other supporters behind them.

The founders of The Evolved Dog and Hope Products International are acting on their own passions, as well as the inspiration of others. Leah's love for dogs led to the creation of her socially conscious company that offers the healthiest and safest products for canines. Lori and her husband saw how their friends were making a difference in the lives of marginalized women in India and couldn't help but put themselves into action to support them.

All of these examples are fueled by passions that run deep within the soul. Adele and her sister wanted to build a school complex in Tanzania so that the girls they'd taught decades before could continue to provide educational opportunities in a developing area. Alysia and Tina wanted to support autistic families, including their own. Bridget and her family wanted to help fill a void for families that had lost an infant.

TAKING ACTION ON YOUR PASSION: ACTION STEPS TO GET YOU STARTED

If you're fired up after reading this chapter, let's get you into action mode. Below are some practical steps and resources to get you started on following your passion.

1. *Find Your Passion*

    Take some time for reflection and figure out what your true passions in life are. If a passion isn't screaming to you, you might use some of the resources below to help discover what you're meant to be doing. Follow that pull and see where it takes you.

2. *Find a Cause That Aligns with Your Passion*

    Before you go out and start your own nonprofit, do some research. Is the work already being done? Could you work with an already existing nonprofit? If the work is not being done, how will you address the problem?

3. *Find a Like-minded Partner (or Mentor)*

   It's not easy to create change in the world alone. In our case studies, those who took action on their passion also had partners and support systems in place. Think about who shares your passion and if a partnership makes sense. Better yet, is there someone who has been through this process and can mentor you? Remember, you won't know unless you ask. Start reaching out to like-minded people and organizations.

4. *Look into Starting a Business or Nonprofit*

   Once you've identified your passion and looked into potential partners and causes, you'll want to think about whether it makes sense to start a traditional business or a nonprofit. There are even some hybrid options to consider. What designation makes the most sense for you and your business? What status will allow you to make the most impact for your cause?

5. *Start Writing a Plan*

   You may be driven by passion to make a change in the world, but you won't get very far without a basic plan in place. Think about your mission, vision, and purpose. What are your short-term and long-term goals? How will you recruit board members? To make change, you need to be clear with your intentions.

TAKING ACTION ON
YOUR PASSION: RESOURCES

Find Your Passion

- "O's 4-Step Guide to Discovering Who You're Meant to Be" from Oprah.com (http://www.oprah.com/spirit/Whats-Your-Passion-Exercise-Find-Your-Passion): "It's about figuring out what you're great at, what it takes to keep you moving forward, and exactly what you need to succeed."

- Five creativity exercises to help you find your passion from Entrepreneur.com (www.entrepreneur.com/article/219709): "Want to start a business, but not sure what to pursue? Here's how to discover what you love."

- "The Short but Powerful Guide to Finding Your Passion" from Leo Babauta (http://zenhabits.net/the-short-but-powerful-guide-to-finding-your-passion): "Following your passion can be a tough thing. But figuring out what that passion is can be even more elusive. And so, in this little guide, I'd like to help you get started figuring out what you'd love doing."

- "3 Simple Ways to Discover Your Passion" from Forbes.com (www.forbes.com/sites/erikaandersen/2012/07/23/3-simple-ways-to-discover-your-passion): "If you've explored a passion possibility in these three ways, and it's appealing to you more than ever—you just may have found your calling."

Find a Cause That Aligns with Your Passion

* "Aligning Your Passion with the Right Cause" from Forbes .com (www.forbes.com/sites/ellengrasso/2010/10/29/aligning -your-passion-with-the-right-cause): "The takeaway here is beware of the paralysis that can set in from overthinking your volunteer efforts. Like the iconic Nike ad implores, 'Just do it.'"

* Charity Navigator website (www.charitynavigator.org): "America's leading independent charity evaluator works to advance a more efficient and responsive philanthropic marketplace by evaluating the Financial Health and Accountability and Transparency of 6,000 of America's largest charities."

* *Cause Marketing for Dummies* (http://www.dummies.com /how-to/content/cause-marketing-for-dummies-cheat -sheet.html): "Your ultimate guide to doing well and good."

Find a Like-minded Partner (or Mentor)

* Search LinkedIn for like-minded people and businesses.
* "How to Find a Business Mentor" from Inc. (www.inc.com /guides/how-to-find-a-business-mentor.html): "Whether you

are just starting out or running a large company, it helps to have a mentor to whom you can turn with questions large and small."

- "Finding a Business Mentor," a list of resources from the U.S. Small Business Administration (www.sba.gov/content/find-business-mentor): "Here are some steps for finding and working with a mentor for your new small business venture."

- "Find Your Next Business Partner Now" from Forbes.com (www.forbes.com/sites/ilyapozin/2012/04/26/find-your-next-business-partner-now): "You may be the most amazing entrepreneur and you could single-handedly build your venture from the ground up, but that doesn't mean you should."

Look into Starting a Business or Nonprofit

- Before starting a nonprofit, consider other business structures from About.com (www.nonprofit.about.com/od/socialentrepreneurs/ss/Before-Starting-A-Nonprofit-Consider-Other-Business-Structures.htm): "There is not a clear line between for-profit and nonprofit organizations when it comes to accomplishing social good. There is, instead, a gradation of business structures to choose from."

- "How to Start a Nonprofit" from the National Council of Nonprofits (www.councilofnonprofits.org/howtostartanonprofit): "One of the most common questions we hear at the

Council of Nonprofits is 'How do I start my own non-profit?' By following the steps below, we hope that many of your questions will be answered."

- "Starting a Nonprofit Organization" from the Society for Nonprofits (www.snpo.org/resources/startup.php): "Questions that we are most commonly asked by individuals who are starting a nonprofit organization."

Start Writing a Plan

- How to Write a Business Plan from the U.S. Small Business Administration (www.sba.gov/category/navigation -structure/starting-managing-business/starting-business /how-write-business-plan): "A business plan is an essential roadmap for business success. This living document generally projects 3–5 years ahead and outlines the route a company intends to take to grow revenues."

- Resources for Nonprofit Financial Management from The Wallace Foundation (www.wallacefoundation.org/knowledge -center/Resources-for-Financial-Management/pages /planning.aspx): "Strong financial management involves four key elements—planning, monitoring, operations and governance. Here are resources for learning how to do them right."

- *Business Planning for Enduring Social Impact: A Social-Entrepreneurial Approach to Solving Social Problems* by An-

drew Wolk and Kelley Kreitz (http://www.rootcause.org
/resources2/business-planning-for-enduring-social-impact-a
-how-to-guide): "*Business Planning for Enduring Social Impact*
applies the strategic rigor and financial savvy of traditional
private-sector business planning to social problem solving."

Giving Model 5:
Giving as a Business Model

*Social impact is the new standard
for how companies address social and
environmental issues to drive meaningful
and positive change.*

From the 2013 Cone Communications
Social Impact Study

Let me be clear about what I mean when I refer to making giving a part of a company's business model. I'm not just talking about Corporate Social Responsibility, or CSR. While every company should have a good CSR program, spelling out self-regulated responsibilities to consumers and the environment does not necessarily mean the company is going above and beyond when it comes to social good. There's a difference between being accountable to shareholders and finding solutions to local and global issues.

Supporting causes through our purchases has become more

popular in the United States in the past few years. Chapter Five laid out several ways in which you can shop with a conscience. We've talked about products and brands that donate proceeds of sales to a cause. Fair trade products ensure equitable wages and living conditions for workers. We can also choose to shop in locally owned businesses or support companies that have demonstrated a commitment to environmentally friendly practices. Let's take the concept of purchasing a step further and consider how we are running our businesses. If you don't run your own business, you might take these giving strategies into consideration when supporting a business; you might even suggest using one of these giving strategies to your boss at work.

Because of the popularity of cause marketing—which is typically defined as the cooperative effort of a for-profit business and a nonprofit organization for mutual benefit—and the desire of American consumers to buy from companies that support good causes, there is an increased need for transparency in businesses that want to give back. While anyone can claim to support a cause, consumers want tangible proof that the money they use to purchase a product is going to have a social impact. As noted in Chapter Two, knowing the impact of giving makes it that more meaningful.

According to the 2013 Cone Communications Social Impact Study, a company's public support of an issue, and to what extent that support is shown, influences personal decisions such as where to shop or what to buy (82 percent) and which products and services to recommend to others (82 percent).[1] The same study found that only 16 percent of consumers felt that companies have made a positive impact on social and environmental issues, and only 25 percent felt that consumers had any power to make a significant impact through their own purchases.

After reading the statistics, you might be wondering how a business, especially a small one, could take on the daunting task of creating a business model that incorporates giving while also remaining viable and competitive. One reason why businesses should make social good a priority is because consumers can be quick to boycott a company whose irresponsible activity is discovered. It is important, then, for a business that takes on a philanthropic role to be transparent about its practices and precise in reporting the impact it is making. It is one thing to say we are making a difference; it is more convincing if we show we are making a difference with our actions.

When people think about companies that incorporate giving into their business model, TOMS shoes often comes to mind. TOMS popularized the One for One model—for every pair of shoes you buy from TOMS, another pair is given to a child in need. The idea came about when founder Blake Mycoskie, while traveling in Argentina, observed that children needed shoes to attend school and protect their feet. Without much knowledge of fashion, shoes, or philanthropy, he created a sustainable business model that helped solve the problem he saw in Argentina. TOMS seems to have inspired many other social enterprises, as you will see from the stories in this chapter.

As I mentioned earlier in this book, all that's required to give back is to have a genuine desire to make a positive impact and then to act on that desire; ideally, this would also inspire others to give and continue the cycle. If you are a business owner, an entrepreneur, or an aspiring entrepreneur, think about that pull you have to give back. Think about your customers and supporters and the products or service you provide. What form of giving makes the most sense for you and your business? What causes or organizations have the same values as you? What can you and your employees, if you have them, handle when you consider the logistics of running a giving program and the potential time and money involved? Is there someone you can partner with to make the giving as seamless as possible for your business? These are just a few questions to consider as you embark on making giving a part of your business model.

Following are six examples of small businesses and entrepreneurs that, often with the help of family and friends, made giving a part of their business model in a way that makes sense to them. You will also find some action steps and resources at the end of the chapter to help you get started on making giving a part of your business model.

THE CENTURY HOUSE[2]

(WWW.THECENTURYHOUSE.COM)

Guests get more than just good accommodations and food at the Century House, a family-owned hotel, restaurant, and conference center in Latham, New York. When guests order an entrée in the dining room, or order food for meetings and weddings, or spend a night in any one of the hotel rooms, the Century House provides one meal in each guest's honor to the Regional Food Bank of Northeastern New York.

The unique program, launched in 2009, is called Enjoy One Share One. Colin Demers, the managing partner at the Century House, came up with the idea as a sustained-giving business model for the company that would also bring together staff and patrons for a good cause. Colin is the nephew of Jim and Dorothy O'Hearn, who opened the hotel and restaurant in the century-old house back in 1949.

As Demers says, the Enjoy One Share One program has

"changed the way the Century House does business." Guests feel good about staying at a hotel that gives back to the local community, and they even share their appreciation by signing a "Book of Giving" at the end of their meal. This book serves as a reminder of each donation made in the guest's honor. In addition, staff members venture out each month to cook and serve at various soup kitchens in the local area. It is in these ways that a culture of giving is created at the Century House for both staff and guests.

At the Century House, guests and staff feel like a family. The Enjoy One Share One Program solidified the establishment's commitment to the community around it.

To date, the Century House has provided more than 500,000 meals through the Enjoy One Share One program.

MITSCOOTS (WWW.MITSCOOTS.COM)

Mitscoots offers socks with a mission using a get + give + employ business model. The company sells 100 percent American-made socks. For every pair sold, Mitscoots gives a pair to someone in need. Mitscoots also employs homeless and other less fortunate people. According to cofounder Tim Scott, starting Mitscoots was a team effort.

Tim and his wife first discovered the value of socks while

volunteering. When talking with homeless people, they found that while food and water were the main needs, socks were a close third. Tim and his wife started to hand out socks and granola bars from their car window while stopped at red lights. At one point, Tim thought that someone should take the TOMS buy one, give one model and use it for socks. But in the meantime, he kept working on his graduate degree and handing out socks from his car window.

After spending some time working as an art director in advertising, he realized how much work he put into trying to convince people to buy one product over another, and he longed to do something that mattered more. It was then that he started toying with his sock idea again. In 2012, Tim came up with a campaign on the crowdfunding site Indiegogo to test out his idea. People loved the concept and the campaign was fully funded, making it possible for Mitscoots to make its first big production run and hire a few individuals in need to help out.

Mitscoots uses the buy one, give one model and takes it a step further by strategically working with organizations that help get people back on their feet through employment, at least on a temporary basis. If these employees can be lifted out of homelessness, they will have the address that is often required to fill out a job application. Mitscoots also uses all American-made materials, keeping profits in the local economy.

In its first two years, Mitscoots has given away ten thousand socks to the homeless. Donations are primarily given to non-profit organizations in the Austin, Texas, area, where Mitscoots is headquartered, but the company will also work with organizations in regions where the socks are selling most. Tim says the company typically employs ten to fifteen people at a time. These employees become a part of the team culture at Mitscoots and are provided with much-needed stability and positive human interaction. The name Mitscoots comes from Tim's early childhood when he would misspell his name as Mit Scoot. That had always been a source of embarrassment for him, but as he explains to his employees, you can take something negative and turn it into a positive.

TIX4CAUSE (WWW.TIX4CAUSE.COM)

Tix4cause is a ticket website with a heart. The tix4cause business model is centered on making a difference and enabling others to easily do so in a very simple, transparent fashion. Every transaction on the website benefits a cause or charity.

The idea for tix4cause came about when founder and CEO Mary Nemetz was at a baseball game with her husband, Kevin. The couple had been involved with charities and giving back since they were children. Looking at the empty seats around them at the baseball game, Mary and Kevin wondered what would happen if people were given the chance to donate their tickets to charity. They started dreaming up ways that would allow those unused seats to raise funds for worthy organizations. They began to work with a company to develop the technology to make tix4cause a reality.

Now with the tix4cause technology, people and businesses with tickets to events that they can't use can donate them to any tix4cause member. When people buy tickets from tix4cause, 90 percent of the purchase price is donated to a selected charity. Athletes and companies have also used tix4cause to donate their unused season tickets to their own foundation or local charities; they can use the tix4cause privacy code feature to control who has access to their tickets.

There is no charge for a charity to be listed on tix4cause, and beneficiaries do not have to be a registered 501(c)(3) nonprofit. For example, causes on the site could include raising funds for a family that can't pay its medical bills. Donors will receive a tax receipt for donations to nonprofit organizations only.

In order to offer a large selection of tickets beyond what's donated, tix4cause partners with a secondary ticket provider that gives them access to 7.5 million tickets every day. Mary tells me that the goal is for everyone to think of tix4cause first when they are searching for an event ticket. They would like for tix4cause to revolutionize the way charities fund-raise and the way people look at entertainment in general.

When I spoke with Mary, she reported that tix4cause was working with more than eight hundred charity members and that the average nondonated ticket transaction yields $26 to the chosen cause. This represents half of what tix4cause earns on a nondonated ticket transaction.

Anyone who uses the tix4cause website becomes a member at no charge. Members can track their activity and see the impact made with their ticket purchases throughout the year. Organizations that are trying to raise funds also have access to customized landing pages that help them market the tickets they are selling for their cause as well as tickets to their own events.

Mary and her team at tix4cause see themselves as bold givers. They are neither ticket brokers nor fund-raisers. They offer technology that partners with charities and donors and purchasers to make a difference. While they offer tickets to sporting events, concerts, theater, and dining and charity events, they want to be the vehicle that people, businesses, and charities use to raise money while also utilizing unused tickets. Since the site went national in 2013, more than $375,000 in proceeds have been donated to charity.

SHARD (WWW.SHARDPOTTERY.COM)

Shard is a coastal lifestyle brand based in Maine that sells dinnerware, mugs, linens, and other gifts with designs capturing the essence of living on the coast of Vacationland. For every product sold by Shard, the company donates a meal to help those in need.

The family-owned business was started by current owner and operator Sunshine Mechtenberg's mother, J. Victoria Rattigan. When Sunshine bought Shard from her mother, she knew she had to ensure the sustainability of the business. It was also important for Sunshine to include a giving component to Shard. While the products offered by Shard were initially all Maine-made, Sunshine saw the opportunity to expand her offerings and reduce her cost by working with manufacturers outside of the United States. Sunshine's mom, an artist, still creates the original artwork for Shard, while Sunshine designs the pieces. She works with a family-owned business in India to produce her linens, and a manufacturer in China that offers good-quality pottery and fair wages to their employees.

Shard has a seasonal location in Bar Harbor and a factory outlet in Freeport. However, Sunshine says the majority of her business comes from wholesalers in the mid-Atlantic region of the United States and Cape Cod, Massachusetts. To keep a local feel to the business, Sunshine makes the meal donations where Shard's products are being sold. If a customer purchases in Maine, the meal donated will be to a local agency in Maine. If a wholesaler is selling Shard's products in Chicago, the meal will be donated in that area. As the Shard website states, "the goal is to create great dinnerware that is perfect for dining tables all over the world, while making a social impact locally."

Since starting the Plate for a Plate giving program in 2012, Shard has donated approximately 25,000 meals, and the number is growing quickly. Sunshine uses a simple meal formula from FeedingAmerica.org or calls nonprofit agencies directly to calculate how much a meal costs in a particular community. Quarterly donations are made to Maine hunger prevention programs such as the Mid Coast Hunger Prevention Program and the Good Shepherd Food Bank, and to other local food banks through Feeding America. When Shard's wholesale customers receive an invoice, they are able to see the impact they have made in their community by selling Shard's products. In turn, each piece of pottery sold comes with a care card and information about the Plate for a Plate program, so the recipients of the beautiful Shard products will also know the purchase had a giving aspect to it.

Shard is still a Maine company at heart, but their social giving component has allowed them to make a great impact on their customers around the United States.

YELLOW LEAF HAMMOCKS[3]

(WWW.YELLOWLEAFHAMMOCKS.COM)

Yellow Leaf Hammocks is a social enterprise and Certified B Corporation focused on bringing people together to enjoy their leisure time while also contributing to the greater good. Yellow Leaf Hammocks believes wholeheartedly that its customers can "Do Good. Relax." and revel in the very best version of multitasking. This "multitasking" can be accomplished by kicking back and relaxing in a "ridiculously comfortable" hammock, which allows Yellow Leaf customers to participate in what the company terms a "hammocking revolution." Purchases of the hammocks, which come in an array of colors and styles, help support sustainable economic opportunity across the globe.

As "Chief Relaxation Officer" Joe Demin puts it, "We're on a mission—not only to help stressed out Americans rejuvenate in the most awesome hammocks on the market, but to build and expand sustainable economic opportunity for marginalized ethnic groups, such as the endangered Mlabri Tribe,

and simultaneously combat deforestation, cultural degrada-
tion and social inequity."

Every Yellow Leaf hammock is 100 percent handwoven by
hill-tribe artisans in rural northern Thailand. The process of
weaving the hammocks can take up to ten days and uses more
than 4 miles of yarn—this makes a big difference in comfort
level when the product is complete. When Yellow Leaf Hammocks first launched in 2011, the company worked with the
Mlabri, a small tribal community that has fought exploitation,
death threats, malnourishment, malaria, and displacement
and was once put on the "Endangered Languages List" by
UNESCO (United Nations Educational, Scientific and Cultural Organization). Joe told me back in 2011 that if his company could sell just two thousand hammocks in the United
States in the next year, they would be able to provide enough
income and work for the entire Mlabri Tribe to escape inden-
tured servitude, end child labor, and leave behind slash-and-
burn deforestation.

Since then, Yellow Leaf has expanded to provide training
and ongoing employment to hill-tribe communities in the
surrounding region as well. The company now employs more
than two hundred weavers, many of whom previously lived on
less than $1 per day. Yellow Leaf has given the Mlabri tribal
community access to training, jobs, and an international mar-

ket, so they now have stable incomes, which has allowed them to invest in a new post office, food service, and sustainable coffee farming. The middle-class wages of the weavers are comparable to that of a college-educated teacher in their region.

In addition to spreading "blissful relaxation" worldwide and empowering artisans at the bottom of the social hierarchy to permanently rise above poverty, Yellow Leaf Hammocks is dedicated to luxury, style, and excellent design. The company has been recognized by *Elle Décor, Architectural Digest, Coastal Living, Vanity Fair*, and *Martha Stewart Living*.

NAJA (WWW.NAJA.CO)

Launched in January of 2014, Naja is a unique lingerie company that makes it possible to change a woman's life by changing the brand of her underwear. Their Underwear for Hope program employs single mothers in the poorest and most violent areas of the world. These women are trained to sew and are given the opportunity to help themselves and their children.

When Catalina Girald started Naja, she knew she wanted to create a brand that empowered women—not just consumers, but the women who made the product as well. While traveling and spending time in remote indigenous communities in western Mongolia, Catalina was struck by one particular difference between the women in the nomadic tribes and the women of the Western world—the tribal women had a tremendous amount of self-confidence. Because their focus was on survival from day to day, they knew exactly what they wanted and understood how to take care of themselves and their families. This experience made Catalina think about the oversexualization of the fashion industry and how it affects the self-esteem of women and girls. But although the women she encountered on her travels may not have had body-image issues perpetuated by the fashion industry, they did lack the economic opportunities to improve their situations.

Catalina decided that she wanted to make a difference through fashion. She saw that 50 percent of lingerie sales came from Victoria's Secret, a company known for their sexualized marketing to young women and girls. She wanted to show women in a different light; lingerie should be about the woman who wears it, making her feel good about herself.

To accomplish Catalina's mission of empowering women through fashion, Naja donates 2 percent of its revenue to educational programs through the Golondrinas Foundation in Colombia. The Underwear for Hope program trains single mothers in the slums of Colombia to sew and then employs them. Because many of these women already have sewing machines in the house, Catalina says the training allows the women to run their own businesses at home, cutting out the employment barriers of transportation and child care. Naja includes a lingerie wash bag, made by the women in the Underwear for Hope program, with all bra purchases. Naja also owns a factory that employs only single mothers or female heads of households. The factory is located in Colombia, where Catalina was born, but she hopes to expand this model to other countries.

Selling luxury lingerie at fair prices is important to Catalina. She not only runs the business but she also designs the lingerie. Producing the products in Colombia allows her to give back to her home country. When I spoke with Catalina, Naja employed thirteen women in the factory and five women in the slums.

MAKING IT HAPPEN

After reading these stories of six inspiring businesses that make giving back an everyday occurrence, I hope you feel less overwhelmed about doing it yourself. As is the case with any of the giving models, there is not one specific way to give.

Rather, your best approach is to assess how you would like to give back as a company and explore ways in which you can take action. The companies you just read about all started out very small, and some remain that way. Regardless, you can still make a significant difference to people and communities locally and globally.

The Century House takes its hospitality focus to the next level by feeding its local community through meal donations and volunteering at soup kitchens. Mitscoots not only donates products to individuals in need but also employs homeless people to make their 100 percent–American-made socks. Tix-4cause partners with a secondary ticket provider to offer event tickets that raise money for a charity or cause. Shard cleverly uses a "plate for a plate" model to donate localized meals when a product of theirs is sold, giving their wholesalers a sense of pride when they sell the products. Finally, both Yellow Leaf and Naja take a global approach by employing and empowering marginalized populations and helping to lift them out of poverty while selling high-quality goods. All of the businesses make giving a part of their business model while also creating a feeling of community with their brands.

GIVING AS A BUSINESS MODEL:
ACTION STEPS TO GET YOU STARTED

Now that you have some inspiration from businesses that make giving back a part of their overall structure, let's take it a step further. Below are five suggested action steps to consider with your business, followed by some resources to help you get started.

1. *Choose a Cause or Organization to Support*

   The first step in making giving part of your overall business is identifying what cause, issue, or organization on which to focus. Ask yourself a few questions: What causes do you, your customers, and your employees care about? Is there a local organization you could partner with? Do you prefer to support a global mission? What makes sense for your business? A clothing retailer supporting a local organization that helps women in need dress for job interviews makes more sense than a fast food restaurant supporting a school obesity program. Be creative!

2. *Figure Out How You Will Give*

   Your giving model does not have to be limited to donating profits. You could choose to donate products, much like the

One for One giving model where you donate a product to someone in need for every one that is sold. You could give specific goods, services, or time. You could choose to employ a population in need. If you do choose to donate profits, you will need to determine how you will calculate the amount to be given and how often. If applicable, you will also need to figure out what will trigger the giving, be it a sale, a milestone, or some other event.

3. *Assess What Your Business Can Handle*

   Once you figure out what cause you want to support and the way in which you want to support it, you will need to figure out how to incorporate that giving without jeopardizing your bottom line. How can you support your cause without interrupting business as usual? Once a giving component is triggered, how is that transaction handled and how often? If you are working with outside organizations or people, how will you communicate with them to ensure the philanthropic deed is being completed as expected? Like anything in business, make sure you have a clear process for your giving.

4. *Consider Your Business Structure*

   Whether you are starting a new business or looking to incorporate giving into an established one, you might want to explore different business designations. Take a look at your business structure and consider the following options that build in social impact and accountability:

- *A low-profit limited liability company (L3C):* L3C is a legal form of business entity in the United States that was created to bridge the gap between nonprofit and for-profit investing by providing a structure that facilitates investments in socially beneficial, for-profit ventures by simplifying compliance with Internal Revenue Service rules.

- *Benefit corporations:* Benefit corporations are a new class of corporation that are required to create a material positive impact on society and the environment and to meet higher standards of accountability and transparency (http://benefitcorp.net/).

- *B Corps:* B Corps are certified by the nonprofit B Lab to meet rigorous standards of social and environmental performance, accountability, and transparency (http://www.bcorporation.net/).

5. *Determine How You Will Measure and Share Your Impact*
   As discussed earlier in the chapter, consumers want to know exactly how businesses are supporting social and environmental causes. As you figure out how to integrate your giving strategy with your business model, it is important to

determine how you will measure the true impact you are making. Consistent and regular reporting will be key for both you and your customers to ensure that you are keeping up with your end of the bargain and that the program is successful. Whether you are reporting on the amount of dollars donated, products given, or people impacted by your work, you will want to quantify it and share it.

GIVING AS A BUSINESS MODEL: RESOURCES

Choose a Cause or Organization to Support

- "3 Simple Ways to Discover Your Passion" (www.forbes.com/sites/erikaandersen/2012/07/23/3-simple-ways-to-discover-your-passion): This article by Erika Andersen on Forbes.com outlines how you can find your genuine passions (not just a hot trend or interest) by examining information, people, and situations to determine your true calling.

- Charity Navigator (www.charitynavigator.org): Charity Navigator provides all-encompassing information about the ins and outs of charities—how popular they are, their financial information, market studies, and so forth. You can browse charities by genre or search for a charity of interest. Charity

Navigator is leading the charge for transparency among charities.

- TED Talks About Passion (www.ted.com/search?cat=ss_all &q=passion): There are a variety of TED Talks focused on the topic of finding your passion. These may help guide you in the direction you want to go.

Figure Out How You Will Give

- *Cause Marketing for Dummies* (http://www.dummies.com /how-to/content/cause-marketing-for-dummies-cheat -sheet.html): This book is chock full of information on how businesses can raise money for nonprofits.

- B1G1 Business for Good (www.b1g1.com/businessforgood): B1G1 is a membership-based company. When your business joins, you can choose which high-impact projects you want to support. As a member, you can use the B1G1 logo and share your impact with your clients or customers. You can also create a gratitude certificate to give to your customers so they know their purchase made a difference. B1G1 helps you measure your impact.

Assess What Your Business Can Handle

- Pledge 1% (www.pledge1percent.org/resources.html): Pledge 1% helps you determine what you can set aside in equity for the community. If you are interested in building a giving program into your company, Pledge 1% can help you determine the financial element of doing this.

- "Finding a Business Mentor" (www.sba.gov/content/find -business-mentor): You may want some help and guidance through this process. Having a mentor is a great way to get both.

- "Create Your Business Plan" (www.sba.gov/category/navigation -structure/starting-managing-business/starting-business/ how-write-business-plan): A business plan is a key element in every business venture, and giving as a business model is no exception.

- The book *Business Planning for Enduring Social Impact: A Social-Entrepreneurial Approach to Solving Social Problems* by Andrew Wolk and Kelley Kreitz (http://www.rootcause .org/resources2/business-planning-for-enduring-social -impact-a-how-to-guide) may help you plan for your nonprofit or giving business structure.

- Find a like-minded partner (www.forbes.com/sites/ilyapozin /2012/04/26/find-your-next-business-partner-now): Perhaps you are not ready to do this on your own. You may want to consider finding a partner with a similar outlook who would be willing to join you in this venture.

Consider Your Business Structure

- Consider other business structures (www.nonprofit.about.com
  /od/socialentrepreneurs/ss/Before-Starting-A-Nonprofit
  -Consider-Other-Business-Structures.htm): Before starting a nonprofit, do your research on other business structures to see if they may fit better with your business.

- B Corps (www.bcorporation.net/become-a-b-corp/how-to
  -become-a-b-corp): Why might you consider becoming a B
  Corp? B Corps are those businesses that want to do something bigger than themselves, like pass legislation, lead a
  movement, participate in a particular campaign, and so
  forth. It makes business sense for them to be established as
  a B Corp. Not every business is eligible for this status. To
  become a certified B Corp, you have to meet certain criteria
  based on achieving a high standard of overall social and
  environmental performance. If you meet both the performance requirement and the legal requirement, you are eligible to proceed through the process.

- Benefit Corp Information Center (www.benefitcorp.net):
  Benefit Corporation is a corporate status legally recognized
  by twenty-six states and the District of Columbia. Benefit
  Corps and B Corps are often confused, but they are quite
  different from each other. Benefit Corporation is a legal

status administered by the state, and the benefit corporation does not need to be certified. B Corporations are certified by the nonprofit B Lab and require a certification as such.

- Going the nonprofit route: There are many great resources to help you if you want to launch your own nonprofit. The Foundation Group (http://www.501c3.org/501c3-services/start-a-501c3-nonprofit/?gclid=CLfU6KDjgrcCFaVcMgodMUAAxA) provides detailed information on starting a 501(c)(3). The National Council of Nonprofits (www.councilofnonprofits.org/howtostartanonprofit) details how to start a nonprofit.

8 Giving Model 6: Giving It Forward

Do what you can, with what you have,
where you are.

Teddy Roosevelt

I talked a lot about *paying it forward* in the chapter on everyday acts of kindness. The term is used to describe how a recipient of a good deed "repays" others by performing another good deed for a different person. This final giving model is the one that ensures that our new simple ways of giving are sustained in the future. I call it *giving it forward* because ideally we are inspiring others to give when we give. There is no obligation to do one particular deed. Instead, we are making sure our everyday actions are modeling good deeds. Whether it's demonstrating giving to our children or writing about giving on our blogs, this chapter will show ways in which you can inspire others to give and make an impact of their own.

While taking the action steps from the giving models illustrated in previous chapters may help you feel happier and more fulfilled in your giving journey, the next question you might ask is, how can we encourage others to do the same? As we discussed earlier, to be most effective in our giving, we aim to inspire others with our acts of giving in order to make giving sustainable over time. One of the easiest ways to do this is by modeling generosity through our actions.

Studies have linked the development of generosity in adults with formative experiences such as seeing family members or other admired people helping others, doing volunteer work, belonging to youth groups, and being helped by others.[1] Raising generous children is simple when you get kids involved with giving at a young age. Talk About Giving, a project of Central Carolina Community Foundation, has shared tips to help parents foster empathy and raise caring kids.[2] Their suggestions include engaging children in activities that benefit others—for example, by encouraging children to share, offering praise for generous behavior instead of rewards (i.e., toys or candy), pointing out the consequences of being unkind to others and discussing how it makes them feel, and modeling behaviors, including concern and support for others. When children see, experience, and are praised for altruistic behavior, they are much more likely to grow up to be giving adults.

I have seen this modeling work with my own children. From the time our children could understand the basic concept of helping others, their father and I have tried to encourage generosity by doing things such as donating food during the holidays, bringing in needed supplies to their daycare without being asked, and, as mentioned earlier, delivering doughnuts to our local fire station. While these were simple activities we could have done individually, we always made an effort to involve our boys. It also helps that their daycare and teachers talk to them about giving to others, and it's no surprise when Gavin tells me, for example, that he has volunteered to bring in Oreos for his holiday party at school and that his class has decided to raise money for the local animal shelter rather than exchange gifts. Or when Biz hands over a freshly made work of art to a tollbooth worker as he pays the fee from the back window during a long trip, making the recipient smile from ear to ear. These generous actions were ideas that an eight year old and a five year old came up with by themselves because they had seen adults in their lives do kind, generous things.

Since starting my blog in 2010, I have a found a tremendously supportive community that reads, comments, and shares my posts. When you write publicly about certain topics over a period of time, such as parenting and social good, you start to attract like-minded people. When you start conversations and develop connections, great things can happen. Blogs and social media can be invaluable in raising awareness for causes in a very personal way. Money can be raised for projects. Volunteers can be found for important work that needs to be done. Problems that happen in our backyard or on a global level can be discussed as if we were all in the same room.

The digital age has allowed philanthropists to share their passion and work for the causes that mean the most to them. Collectively, bloggers, readers, advocates, parents, teens, and everyday people can use their voices to make a difference in local and global development. While I was in Nicaragua for a week with WaterAid America and had very little access to the Internet, we were still able to generate 1,800 tweets, reaching 2 million Twitter accounts with more than 10 million impressions and nearly 300 interested bloggers. Our Twitter chat on World Water Day raised awareness for the sheer lack of clean water and sanitation that exists in our world.

You can still give it forward even without children or a social media platform. Our everyday actions say a lot about who we are as people. Thus far, we've talked about how giving makes us feel good and how we can incorporate more giving into our lives, whether it be through kind acts, donating time or money, shopping with a conscience, taking action on our passions, or incorporating giving into our businesses. This chapter is about walking the walk while also talking the talk. Your self-awareness, when it comes to your giving habits, is key to this more subtle giving model. The following stories illustrate how passionate people are giving on their own time in their own unique ways. They give because they have something to offer, not because they want recognition. The impact that they are making keeps them going.

MOM BLOGGERS FOR SOCIAL GOOD[3]

(WWW.MOMBLOGGERSFORSOCIALGOOD.COM)

Jennifer James started blogging back in 2004—at a time when most people had never even heard the term *blog*. In 2007, she founded the oldest and largest social network dedicated to mom bloggers in the world, Mom Bloggers Club. Clearly ahead of her time in terms of leveraging the power of social media and creating online communities, Jennifer has had a unique perspective in seeing how mom bloggers, in particular, have grown throughout the years. From sharing stories about theirs kids to working with the largest brands in the world, mom bloggers have come a long way in terms of making their voices heard.

It was around Christmas of 2011 that Jennifer had the idea of harnessing the power of mom bloggers to create a community for social good. She already had a network of bloggers and wondered if they would be open to writing and using their social media influence for good. The idea was sparked by her reflections on a trip to Kenya, her first time out of the United States, with ONE.org and ten other mom bloggers in July of 2011. The purpose of the trip was to see programs funded by the U.S. government, which included health care clinics that worked with mothers, smaller hospitals that helped children, CDC programs, and some cultural programs. Jennifer describes the trip as life changing.

In January 2012, Mom Bloggers for Social Good was created. This new platform, which partners with nonprofits and NGOs around the world, gave bloggers a means of spreading the word about social good initiatives. Jennifer makes it simple for members to participate by sending out information via the blog that is easy to share on Twitter or Facebook.

Jennifer found out quickly that her community of mom bloggers was more than ready to embrace social good. She started getting e-mails from people who wanted to do more. They wanted to understand and tackle the issues and get more involved with the partners and initiatives. That's when the Global Team of 200 was created.

The Global Team of 200 (www.globalteamof200.tumblr .com), of which I am a member, is a highly specialized group of members of Mom Bloggers for Social Good that concentrates on issues involving women and girls, children, world hunger, and maternal health. Members commit to writing at least two posts per month for the teams and its partners. The motto of the Global Team of 200 is "Individually we are all powerful. Together we can change the world. We believe in the power of collective action to help others and believe in ourselves to make this world a better place for our children and the world's children."

Mom Bloggers for Social Good and the Global Team of 200 are all-volunteer efforts, and their voices are being heard around the world. According to Jennifer, the more than 3,000 members' social media shares and blog posts have reached 50 million people worldwide.

Nonprofits and NGOs are excited about working with the global team and social good moms in general. They see a group of highly intelligent women who care and have the influence to make a big impact with their messages that often include their own personal stories and perspectives. In addition to blogging and social media partnerships, Jennifer has worked with several NGOs to coordinate insight trips for bloggers in order to replicate the experience she had with ONE.org. Jennifer and members of the Global Team of 200 have visited India, Zambia, Tanzania, South Africa, Indonesia, the Philippines, and Nicaragua. These trips give members the unique opportunity to report on global health and development programs on the ground with Mom Bloggers for Social Good partners in low- and middle-income countries.

Getting involved with this global coalition of mothers who care is as easy as filling out a simple contact form online (www.mombloggersforsocialgood.com/are-you-a-mom-blogger-your-voice-matters-join-us). All you need is an e-mail and a blog.

LETICIA BARR (TECHSAVVYMAMA.COM) + DAUGHTER EMILY (RIBBONBARRETTES.COM)

Leticia Barr, founder of the blog Tech Savvy Mama, first visited Haiti in 2012. Two years after the earthquake of 2010 hit, Leticia was struck by the devastation that remained there. Her father-in-law had visited the country in the 1980s and encouraged her to visit. He told her that despite the political unrest in Haiti, the country was beautiful and the people were warm. Leticia knew there was more to Haiti's story than what the mainstream media reported. As a former teacher, she also knew that traveling can be the best form of learning.

By February 2015, Leticia had made her fourth trek to Haiti. She went on behalf of Everywhere, a social media and marketing agency, to visit the Artisan Business Network artists who create products for the Macy's Heart of Haiti line. She brought along her eleven-year-old daughter, Emily. Although it wasn't the first time Emily got her passport stamped, this special trip to Haiti was her first visit to a developing country. (See Chapter Five for more on the Artisan Business Network.)

Leticia had already planted a seed in Emily's mind after her own first trip to Haiti. She took Emily to social-minded conferences and talked with her about how kids can take the initiative in giving. Emily was inspired by a glove drive she heard her friend and classmate Melia speak about at Elena Sonnino's Moms+Tweens+Social Good in D.C. The drive collected gloves and mittens from every state. After learning how to make ribbon barrettes at the Digital Summit blogging conference, Emily set up a table at her local pool where she sold the barrettes and raised $142 in one summer.

Leticia encouraged Emily when she saw how proud her daughter was of the money she raised. Emily donated the money to support her friend, Ava, who lives with cystic fibrosis, and made a goal to raise even more money the next summer. Leticia used her social media platform to share what Emily was doing, and people started to ask questions and put in orders. Soon Leticia and Emily were setting up a Facebook page and website. Ribbon Barrettes for Research was created, and 100 percent of all sales benefit the Cystic Fibrosis Foundation. Emily has already raised more than $2,500 since June 2014 for her chosen cause. Leticia says she supports Emily when she needs it and backs off when she needs to take a break.

After seeing her mom visit Haiti multiple times, Emily asked if she could go, too. Leticia weighed the risks and decided she felt comfortable taking her daughter. She wanted Emily to see that there was more to the country than what people hear about in the news. The trip was eye-opening for Emily. She noticed that the people had houses just like her. She had expected to see more people living in the tent villages that were prevalent after the earthquake. She also noticed many commonalities between Haitians and Americans and was inspired by the artist communities she visited.

In Emily's words, "People should go to Haiti because even though it's very close to the United States, it's very different. It gives you a perspective on how we worry about things that aren't so important. In Haiti, people worry about having work to buy food and support their families. Visiting Haiti helps create jobs for everyone and brings awareness about what a great country it is and how we can help."

Emily brought her barrettes with her to Haiti and got an order for more than forty, making her company international in scope. Leticia says Emily is already planning her next trip.

Bringing Emily to Haiti was an investment in her future as a global citizen.

MAINE'S ANGELS

(WWW.FACEBOOK.COM/MAINESANGELS)

Maine's Angels make homemade angel and blessing gowns for infants who are dying or have passed. The gowns are lovingly made by volunteers from donated formal wear such as wedding dresses and then given to local hospitals.

Nicole, who prefers to remain anonymous on the Maine's Angels Facebook page, began making angel gowns after the passing of her own infant. In 2011, she lost one of her twins at just twenty-five days due to a rare disease that only affects identical twins in the womb called twin-to-twin transfusion syndrome (TTTS). Nicole recalls receiving two gowns when her daughter Elli died, a cremation gown and an angel gown. As Nicole shared with me, "Honestly, it was nice having something to put my girls in. We had clothes, but they were way too big, and nothing we had was good enough for the occasion."

Nicole says she was very calm the whole time. She and her husband were able to dress their daughter and spend some time with her before saying good-bye. To a certain extent, it was a relief to not see her tiny baby naked with tubes and wires attached to her body. Nicole was thankful to have had the ability to hold her daughter, even for a short time, and dress her like a "real mom" would. On that day, they dressed Elli, loved her, anointed her and her twin sister, and then placed them together. Nicole saw that the gowns made the pictures that much more memorable and easier to handle—it meant someone else would see her child as a child and not just a dead baby.

This difficult experience in the hospital led Nicole to start Maine's Angels. In her heart, she knew that she hadn't been the only one to take care of Elli in the short period she was alive. The gown reminds her that someone took the time, love, and effort to give something that Elli would not otherwise have. The perfect fitting gown provided meaning and beauty during what Nicole describes as an ugly time. She wanted to share this comfort with others, to give to other "loss moms" in their most desperate time of need—a need that wasn't being fulfilled in Maine.

Before starting Maine's Angels in 2014, Nicole had never used a sewing machine. Then she used her grandmother's old machine until she cracked a gear in it and had to buy another. She taught herself to make the gowns and now offers occasional free workshops to teach others to do so. The operation is completely volunteer-run and the gowns are made during

Nicole's free time. She has the help of other volunteers who take apart donated dresses and sew the gowns.

The process for donating to Maine's Angels is simple. There are three locations for people to drop off donated wedding dresses and formal wear. The dresses are then picked up by Nicole and sent off to be dismantled. The pieces of the dresses, veils, and accessories are then lovingly put together to create the angel gowns and wraps. The entire process is documented in photos and shared on Maine's Angels Facebook page. Each donated piece receives a name, such as the Jennifer I collection, so that donors can see how their contribution has been used. It is a powerful and meaningful sight to see and experience. The finished pieces are donated to three local hospitals. Nicole would also like to work with funeral homes in the future.

Nicole admits to breaking down in tears each time she receives a donation. She does not want recognition for the gowns, since it is part of her grieving process. It is a bittersweet process, but she understands what it is like to be on the receiving end of such a gown.

NO HOLDING BACK (KATBIGGIE.COM)

The No Holding Back blog is one that has blossomed into a rich platform for advocacy and social good. Like Maine's Angels, Alexa Bigwarfe started the blog after the loss of one of her infant twin daughters due to complications from TTTS in 2011. Her goal was to have a place to grieve, but she also felt the need to raise awareness of the syndrome that took her daughter and to talk about maternal and infant health in general.

Over time, Alexa has used No Holding Back to advocate for causes close to her heart, like advocacy for prematurity awareness, childhood health, and hunger in children. She is a huge advocate and fund-raiser for the March of Dimes and tries to write regularly about prematurity and neonatal care, using her own experience as her guide. If it impacts the health of women and children, Alexa is motivated to write about the topic.

While blogging about her loss, Alexa began to receive e-mails and comments from others who were also hurting from the loss of a pregnancy, baby, or child. When a friend delivered her baby girl stillborn at 38 weeks, Alexa felt the need to do even more. While watching her friend grieve, she desperately wanted to be able to provide her friend with the knowledge and hope that one day things would get better again, much like they did for her. Alexa decided to gather stories from other parents who lost babies and children and to compile them into a book of survival tips for grieving parents. The book, *Sunshine After the Storm: A Survival Guide for the Grieving Mother*, was published in October 2013, just in time for Pregnancy and Infant Loss Awareness Day.

Alexa did not stop with her blog, advocacy work, and survival guide. Once the book was published, Alexa still felt the pull to do more. She could see that sharing her story and the stories of other grieving mothers was making an impact. She wanted to get *Sunshine After the Storm* into as many hands as possible and did not want mothers to have to buy it, so she launched a nonprofit organization to support grieving parents called Sunshine After the Storm, Inc. The purpose of this 501(c)(3) organization is to raise the funds to donate copies of the book to hospitals, bereavement groups, and individuals who are suffering from the loss of a child. To date, the book has been donated to more than five hundred people and has received rave reviews—it is described as just what is needed at just the right time. Alexa and a group of grieving mothers regularly visit local hospitals in the Columbia, South Carolina, area to deliver copies of the book and other bereavement materials in person.

Alexa launched the website Sunshine After the Storm

(http://sunshineafterstorm.us) to support her nonprofit in 2013. The site includes resources for grieving parents and those who are trying to support them, request forms for copies of the book, and a platform for raising money for the organization. As donations are received, copies of the book are provided to parents in need. Alexa has also started sending bereavement packages along with the book because she knows how important those loving packages are for a mother going through the very worst situation she could imagine. She considers these packages to be a hug from afar.

Sharing her story and helping other grieving mothers not only helps Alexa heal from her own loss but also allows her to show others they are not alone.

LEAD SAFE AMERICA FOUNDATION
(LEADSAFEAMERICA.ORG)

When Tamara Rubin found out in 2005 that her children had tested positive for lead poisoning after a home renovation that involved an open flame torch to remove exterior paint, she knew she had to do something. As Tamara puts it, she was "mad as hell." She wanted to spread the word about the dangers of lead poisoning and teach others how to test for lead and prevent more children from getting sick.

Lead poisoning is a common problem in America. It is irreversible, preventable, and not often talked about. Between 2008 and 2010, Tamara took her message to the mass media in order to reach middle- and lower-income audiences in particular. She told her story on platforms including the *Today Show* and *USA Today*, but found that she was still frustrated that she wasn't making enough of a difference. She then started a personal website, www.mychildrenhaveleadpoisoning .com. The website helped Tamara formalize her advocacy work and create a platform for education and resources on lead poisoning. She also used the website to send out free lead-testing kits. She would even host "testing parties" where she would test toys for attendees so they could learn just how safe their children were in their everyday activities.

Seeing that her message was getting out and that it was making an impact, Tamara established Lead Safe America Foundation (LSAF) as a nonprofit organization in 2011. LSAF's mission is to protect children from hazards created by lead found in their homes, schools, child-care centers, playgrounds, parks, and the environment. Its programs include emergency intervention and support for families whose children have been poisoned, outreach and education for the prevention of childhood lead poisoning, and parent advocate support to encourage parents who want to help spread the word. Tamara's original goal was to help one hundred people in LSAF's first year, but she ended up helping more than a thousand. In 2014, LSAF helped more than sixteen thousand families.

LSAF is a volunteer-run organization that relies on support through donations. To further spread her message about the dangers of lead poisoning, Tamara created a documentary film called *MisLEAD: America's Secret Epidemic*. Filming for the documentary started in December 2011, and a rough-cut was completed in January 2014. The film project is 100 percent supported by donations through LSAF and is planned for release in theaters. Tamara's ultimate goal is to have a finished film, a fully funded foundation, and satellite offices around the country where she can hire moms who have stayed home with lead-poisoned children so that they can be reintroduced into the workplace.

KIOO PROJECT[4] (WWW.KIOOPROJECT.ORG)

Babita Patel's mother always taught her that whenever you have the ability to help someone, you should do it without hesitation or expectation of anything in return. This lesson, passed down from her grandfather, keeps Babita going when she becomes overwhelmed with the work she does as executive director of the nonprofit she cofounded, KIOO Project (formerly View Finder Workshop).

Babita is a professional humanitarian photographer whose work with nonprofits and NGOs has taken her all around the globe. It was common for curious children to run up to her as she photographed on location. Though she was protective of her expensive equipment at first, she would humor the kids by taking photos of them and letting them look at the pictures on the camera's screen. One ten-year-old child, who lived in a slum in Haiti, giggled when he came to the photo of himself. He knew it was a photo of him because it was the only person in the sequence of photos that he did not recognize, and the child was wearing the same shirt that he had on. Babita was astounded that he was seeing himself for the very first time in his life.

"I was struck dumb," she tells me. "For I never realized a person could walk through life without knowing his own physical self. But photography can change that. It lets a child see himself and his world through different eyes. By learning tangible skills and creating new avenues of self-expression, he can contribute to his life and his community."

This experience made Babita realize that there was something more she could do with her talents as a photographer.

She asked herself the question, What happens if I give children the camera and allow them to create their own photography?

Babita created View Finder Workshop in 2013 to help disadvantaged children learn self-expression, self-confidence, and self-worth through photography. Looking through a viewfinder helps children see themselves and their world differently. Literally. View Finder Workshop was renamed KIOO Project in September 2014. KIOO, pronounced "KEY-oh," is the Swahili word for *mirror*, connoting the idea of reflection and the power a child can get when she discovers who she is.

Babita has held workshops with eighteen child slaves in Haiti and forty-two children and four teachers in the slums of Nairobi, Kenya. As Babita notes, studies have shown that tapping into children's creative potential will help them with their math and science classes, improve their problem-solving skills, and grow them into future leaders within their communities. A gallery show exhibiting the children's work is held at their respective schools at the end of the weeklong workshop. All the equipment is then donated to the school, so the students can continue their photography education long after the workshop is over. KIOO Project has also hosted gallery showings of the children's work in New York City and Santa Monica, California.

The photography workshops, which explore self-identity

and community-identity, give the children new perspectives on who they are, especially within their neighborhood, through photography. Babita has noticed that girls respond the most to taking self-portraits, while the boys like showing who they are by photographing the things that appeal to them. She was particularly struck by a girl in Kenya named Jane who was engaged with all of Babita's assignments except for the one on self-portraits. When Jane said she was not beautiful, Babita helped Jane feel more comfortable taking photos of herself by finding the items and colors that made Jane happy. At the end of the assignment, Babita was brought to tears when Jane noted in the caption of her self-portrait that the assignment and the encouragement of three friends helped her realize that she is beautiful.

Babita admits that taking on such a big project, which involves a lot of planning and travel, can be daunting. She has embraced the challenge and has learned from the stumbling blocks that she has had in the past. When she is tempted to quit, she thinks about what would happen if she stopped. KIOO Project is working to solidify strategic partners that will help support future workshops, which thus far have been funded mainly through crowdfunding sources and individual donations. These partnerships will allow KIOO Project to offer its life-changing workshops to marginalized children around the world. After all, everyone deserves the opportunity to unleash their creativity, recognize and celebrate their individuality, and explore their lives through a different lens.

MAKING IT HAPPEN

How often do we do a good deed for others and keep it to ourselves? While anonymity can make an act of kindness more powerful, we can make giving more sustainable by sharing the story with our children and others. Something as simple as taking your kids to volunteer with you can make a difference. Sharing the way we give and how it makes us feel can be the best gift we give to others.

Babita shared with me how she has thought about quitting the KIOO Project because it requires so much work. But the impact she has on children who are seeing themselves for the first time is worth taking the extra time for strategic planning. The same can be said for both Alexa and Nicole, as they tirelessly work to help grieving mothers feel whole again. By sharing the experience of visiting a developing country with her daughter, Leticia is molding a future global citizen. Jennifer was so moved by her experience in Kenya with ONE.org that she has dedicated herself to replicating the experience for other mothers who blog and empowering them to use their voices for social good. Mom Bloggers for Social Good is not the platform that makes Jennifer money, but she is the most dedicated to it. Tamara will not stop her crusade against lead poisoning in America as long as there are still dangers out there for children.

All of the stories in this chapter illustrate everyday people giving in a way that is meaningful and personal to them. They are involving others through gallery shows, blogging, social media, travel, film, and grassroots advocacy. Having met these women, I can also say that none of them do what they do to get attention or a pat on the back. They deeply want to help and inspire others through their actions.

GIVING IT FORWARD:
ACTION STEPS TO GET YOU STARTED

Now that you understand the concept of giving it forward, it's time to think about how you can make your giving more sustainable over time by inspiring others with your actions. Following are a few ways you might approach giving it forward in your own life.

1. *Dig Deep and Reflect on How You Give*

   The first step to giving it forward is to understand how you give in the first place. You don't have to have a blog or a project like you read about in the stories in this chapter. Maybe you volunteer regularly at a local nonprofit or foster shelter dogs. Even taking the time to check in on an elderly neighbor or collecting empty bottles and cans for a youth group is an inspiring way to give. The key is to be aware of how you give so you can share it.

2. *Think About Ways to Share Your Experiences*

How can others get involved with your giving? Can you bring them along with you? Can they contribute in some way? Think about ways in which those around you, both physically and virtually, can participate. This gives others a way to truly understand how you give and why. Children, especially, benefit from early exposure to acts of giving.

3. *Talk About Your Giving*

If people can't participate in your giving directly, be sure to tell them about it. Have conversations about the causes you are most passionate about at dinner parties, read books about giving to your kids, start discussions on your blog or Facebook page. You will get the best results when you focus on how your giving has impacted you personally.

4. *If You Are Looking to Start a Project or Organization, Begin with the Big Picture and Move Backward*

Babita, executive director of KIOO Project, shared how she approached planning something as big as her photography workshops in faraway developing countries. She started with her big goal of hosting a workshop and then went backward until she got to the first step. In order to hold the workshop, she had to make travel arrangements to the country. Before that, she had to fund-raise. Moving backward from the big goal makes it less daunting.

5. *Walk the Walk*

Whether you share and inspire through your current giving or start something new, the important piece of the equation is that you are actually giving. The best and most effective way to start giving it forward is to actually go forth and give! Join the Mom Bloggers for Social Good, volunteer with your kids, donate proceeds of the sales in your company to charity, get out and do something for someone else that makes you feel impassioned. When you walk the walk, people will automatically see how giving affects you in a positive way and then be inspired by it.

GIVING IT FORWARD: RESOURCES

• Talk About Giving (www.talkaboutgiving.org/resources): This website has a great resources page that includes curricula and programs for children and families on giving and raising generous kids.

- Become a member of ONE.org (www.one.org/us/take -action/dashboard): ONE is an international campaigning and advocacy organization that helps more than 6 million people take action—in the form of petitions, letters, phone calls, and local events—to end extreme poverty and preventable disease, particularly in Africa.

- Join Mom Bloggers for Social Good (www.mombloggers forsocialgood.com/are-you-a-mom-blogger-your-voice -matters-join-us): The more moms who are part of Mom Bloggers for Social Good, the more good can be done through our blogs and social media.

- Join The Mission List (www.themissionlist.com): Members of The Mission List use their social media influence to impact social good at home and abroad through social good campaigns involving issues such as child and maternal health, global development, women's rights, and hunger.

9 Become a Simple Giver

*I believe great people do things
before they are ready.*

Amy Poehler

I'm going to make the assumption that you understood the value of giving before picking up this book. Why else would you get a book called *Simple Giving*? You don't have to study the psychological aspects of giving to know that it simply feels good to give. It also feels pretty darn good to be on the receiving end of a good deed, which often makes you want to spread even more good in the world.

Authors and sociologists Christian Smith and Hilary Davidson reported that those Americans who volunteered an average of 5.8 hours per month described themselves as being "very happy," while those who only volunteered 0.6 hours per month labeled themselves as "unhappy."[1] The findings of their comprehensive study on all aspects of American generosity are compiled in their book *The Paradox of Generosity*. Lower depression rates were found among Americans who donated more than 10 percent of their incomes. In addition, it was found that those who are very giving in relationships—being emotionally available and hospitable— are more likely to be in "excellent health" (48 percent) than those who are not (31 percent).

Finding a meaningful life, as described by positive psychologist Martin Seligman, involves using our strengths to serve something that is larger than ourselves. To weave giving into our lives brings us the added benefits of feeling happier and healthier. Why wouldn't we want to give more?

Of course, it can be difficult to make giving a top priority when we have so many other things competing for our attention. We live full lives that involve a number of responsibilities—whether in the areas of work, school, parenting, taking care of loved ones, socializing, or extracurricular activities. I know there are days when I feel like I never stop moving. To become a simple giver means identifying and acting upon the opportunities presented in everyday life. It's up to you to find the opportunities that make the most sense for you given your schedule and passions; think about where you find the most joy and meaning.

In the first chapter, I explained my pull to give. My journey started when I began to explore the concept of philanthropy through my blog. I looked at different definitions of *philanthropy* and *giving*; searched for stories of those who incorporated giving into their everyday lives, which I shared on my blog; started my own personal giving pledge; and studied the psychology behind giving. I am still on this journey—I am not sure it is one that ever stops. As we grow and learn from our experiences, and as our lives evolve, it makes sense that our giving will also change. There are times when we can give more of ourselves, our time, and our money, and there will be times when we have to step back and take a break.

Stepping back and evaluating what we are doing to give and whether or not we are making the impact we want are key. There is no right or wrong way to do any of this because giving is such a personal experience. Our passions are different. The results we want to see are different. How we ultimately choose to give will be different.

It's time to go back to the questions I asked you in that first chapter. Think, again, about why you picked up this book in the first place. You might have wanted to learn about ways in which you could give. Maybe you experienced a pull to give and just weren't sure how to act upon it. Now that you've gone through the book, think about the giving models or stories that resonated most deeply with you.

- What moves you to give?
- What kind of legacy do you want to leave?
- How can you incorporate some of these giving models into your own life?
- What is feasible for you to try right now?

Remember, this is a journey. If you go off course or make a wrong turn, you can simply try a new route.

If you've read this book from cover to cover, going through each giving model successively, you may have noticed that there is some overlap in the application of each model. In fact, there are many stories from this book that could fit into more than one chapter. One does not have to limit oneself to choosing one model. You might create a company with a business model that incorporates giving, while also making it a point to perform random acts of kindness and shop consciously on a regular basis with your children. The sky is the limit when it comes to giving.

While we're reviewing, let's take another look at the broader definition of giving I proposed in the first chapter. To give back in a meaningful way, I believe you need two key components:

1. A person should genuinely want to make a positive impact.
2. The act should benefit someone or something else.

Ideally, to be most effective in your philanthropic deeds over time, you also want to strive for two other key components:

1. The act should inspire others to do their own giving.
2. You want to make your giving sustainable over time.

We also talked about the three ways to get the most out of your giving: choice, connection, and impact. We get more satisfaction when the act of giving is our choice, when we can give to a person or cause we feel connected to, and when we know the gift makes a specific impact. With this knowledge base and a little self-reflection, we can each start to come up with our very own simple giving strategy.

My hope is that after reading this book, you will not only have a broader understanding of what it means to give but you will also be more mindful of opportunities to give on a regular basis. My intention is to help make giving an everyday habit, and not because you feel like you *have* to or because it's the right thing to do, but because it makes us and everyone around us happy. Because we understand we can help others with more than just a monetary donation or volunteering an hour here and there at a local nonprofit. Because we can change the world with our actions.

SIGNS YOU'VE BECOME A SIMPLE GIVER

My main reason for writing this book was to dispel the myth that being philanthropic requires having a lot of time and money. This is simply not true. There are many ways to make giving a natural part of your life. As illustrated in the stories, everyday people are making change in the world in their own unique ways.

I've been interviewing people for my Philanthropy Friday series for about four years. I can honestly say that each and every person has inspired me in a different way. While I may not be able to replicate what each person does to give back, the passion for what they do is palpable. When you find that place where giving is so easy that you're not thinking about it, you know you are a simple giver.

I found the perfect giving opportunity in volunteering for my local BackPack Program, where I help pack bags with food so local school kids have enough nourishment during the weekends. It was a new program to the area, and the weekly volunteer slots filled up quickly. I went online and signed up for as many Tuesday evenings as I could throughout the school year. I went by myself at first, thinking I didn't want to deal with the hassle of bringing my kids. Plus, it was my time to volunteer. I had been searching for a place to volunteer close to home, but I hadn't found anything that appealed to me until I heard about the BackPack Program. I couldn't imagine how tough it must be for kids to rely on school for food. I'd be helping to nourish the peers of my own children. For some reason, it didn't occur to me that they might want to help, too.

At some point, I had to bring my kids with me to volunteer because I couldn't find child care. It stressed me out to have to keep an eye on a five year old and an eight year old as we organized crates for each school, unloaded the week's menu items, and filled bags on an assembly line. However, I found out quickly that my boys were not only more than capable of helping but that they also wanted to help out. They could help tape labels on the crates, put food into the bags, and replenish items that people on the assembly line were running out of. My youngest's favorite job was "squishing" the empty boxes after the food items were emptied out of them. The other volunteers were more than welcoming to them. Other kids would show up with their parents every now and then as well, giving them some playmates.

After my husband and I divorced, it was easier to take my boys with me to volunteer than to arrange for a babysitter. We are on our second year of volunteering for the BackPack Program, and my oldest son is at the point where he can actually lead the volunteers if our regular leader is absent. He helps new volunteers get acclimated and makes sure our assembly line is always running smoothly. My youngest steps into the assembly line and squishes boxes every now and then.

Along the way, we have met some really great people while volunteering. They have become our friends, making our twice-per-month commitment even more enjoyable. The boys also know that they are helping kids in their own schools. They understand how lucky we are to have healthy meals every day.

Volunteering can feel like a burden sometimes. We have busy lives, and our time is precious. But when you find a good fit, where you can work alongside good souls and feel fulfilled from the work you are doing, it's truly magical. My boys look forward to our volunteering time, and they appreciate that we are doing it to help their peers. This is simple giving at its best, if you ask me.

PULLING IT ALL TOGETHER

As I was wrapping up the writing of this book, I had an experience that I couldn't possibly leave out. It completely encapsulated all of the aforementioned giving models in a one-hour time period on a cold Sunday morning at my very nontraditional gym, WolfPack Fitness, in Auburn, Maine.

Just eleven days before World Water Day, which is held on March 22 every year, I had messaged my trainer and the founder of WolfPack Fitness, Luke Robinson, to see if he would be willing to use our regular Primal Fitness class to raise awareness for the global water and sanitation crisis. Our large group class (open to the public and all fitness levels) is held every Sunday at 9:00 a.m., and World Water Day just happened to fall on a Sunday. Luke would always incorporate a story into our weekly workouts. We would break into groups of four and work through several different stations that would creatively tell a story. My idea was to tell a water story.

Given that Luke is incredibly open-minded and creative, it was no surprise that it took him all of one minute to get back to me and tell me he was in. The next day, I told him more about my insight trip to Nicaragua with WaterAid America the year before and why World Water Day was important to me. I gave him some ideas I had for stations to tell our water story and sent him photos from my trip as inspiration. We decided to donate any proceeds from the class to WaterAid America. The plan was simple—I would coordinate with WaterAid America, and Luke would take care of planning the workout.

My friends at WaterAid America let me know about #Blue4Water, a hashtag they were using to encourage people to wear blue on World Water Day to raise awareness for the cause on social media. Luke posted a notice about this in our World Water Day Primal Fitness event page, and I posted about my experience and why the day was important to me. People responded immediately.

I should also mention that we do these Sunday-morning workouts outside year-round in Maine. Yes, even in the dead of winter. We've had wonderful workouts in the snow and on the frozen Androscoggin River. If the elements are too extreme or messy, we move into an unheated barn, where we've comfortably fit more than forty people. On the morning of World Water Day, the wind was whipping and the temperatures were low. The "feels like" temperature was -1° when I woke up.

Yet we still had more than forty people show up, wearing blue. Luke took the time to show on a screen in the unheated barn some of my Nicaragua photos that inspired our workout stations. He gave me the chance to say a few quick words about World Water Day and my time with WaterAid America in Nicaragua. After explaining the eleven stations that would tell our water story, we danced to "Splish Splash (I Was Taking a Bath)" to warm up, then did our workout. We mimicked things like pumping a well and carrying water back to the village while holding the hand of a child. At the end, we donated $300 to WaterAid America, supporting a WASH (WAter, Sanitation and Hygiene) program in schools in Nicaragua.

As I wrote for a ONE.org blog post about the experience, WolfPack Fitness is "a community of supportive, caring members who embrace new people and ideas with open arms. We make things happen. Together."[2] I'm not sure anyone would have known it was World Water Day had I not asked Luke if we could commemorate it. I knew Luke and the entire community he has created would be open to the idea because we support one another in so many ways, whether it's encouraging each other to deadlift heavier weight, cooking dinners for a woman who just had her third baby, or volunteering at a local farm.

We were also in the middle of what we were calling 40 Days of Giving when the World Water Day Primal Fitness event happened. The 40 Days of Giving was an idea from another WolfPack Fitness member who wanted to give for forty days instead of giving something up for Lent. Luke made an event page, and community members were encouraged to come up with their own ideas of how they wanted to give. No idea was too big or too small. As you can see, my World Water Day idea fit in well with this community.

The event had a great turnout, but it was also successful in that I was able to bring a caring community, to which I already belonged, into a global conversation. They left feeling great because of the workout and because they were taking part in something meaningful. Of course, it was meaningful to me because I had the opportunity to share my passion for a cause with a large group of people whom I cared about. We posted beautiful photos and video from our water-themed workout on social media and inspired others with our creative advocacy.

Depending on the weather, the commute to WolfPack Fitness takes me forty-five minutes to an hour. I've made a conscious decision to make this commute because there is no other place like WolfPack near me. The company is committed to natural movement and uses nontraditional weights such as cinderblocks. There is no talk of a scale, unless we're talking about ditching it. What keeps me coming back is the supportive, caring community and the fact that Luke is committed to giving back. Luke often donates proceeds from his regular large-group workouts to charity, usually at the suggestion of a member. It is not uncommon for an act of kindness to happen before, during, or after a workout. Luke's passion for what he does as a trainer and nutritionist is clearly evident. He goes above and beyond to make everyone's experience as meaningful as possible. By sharing our experiences and photos in the community and on social media, we inspire others to take their commitment to their overall health and the health of those around them a step further.

MAKING IT HAPPEN

My World Water Day experience made me realize that you could actually experience all six giving models at once while doing something as simple as working out. I've said time and time again that I am on my own philanthropic journey. When I started to be more conscious about giving, I found that opportunities to give just came to me. I would have never thought I'd be giving back by committing to make myself stronger, but I am. When I first signed up for my local BackPack Program, I didn't anticipate how much I would be teaching my children. Pledging to donate to a different charity each month showed me why and how I give and made it more of a habit. Writing my Philanthropy Friday series connected me to so many different people and resources that opened my mind to new ways of giving back.

We all have opportunities to give in our lives. Sometimes they're not as obvious as we'd like, but the opportunities exist. After reading this book, you may realize that you are actually giving more than you'd thought. I have no doubt that you are.

If you have performed a random act of kindness or chosen to buy fair trade products at a local shop in your neighborhood, you are already a simple giver! If you're like me and feel you could do more to give, now is the time to reflect on the giving models and inspirational stories and start mapping out your own simple giving strategy.

BECOME A SIMPLE GIVER: FIVE ACTIONS STEPS TO CREATE YOUR OWN SIMPLE GIVING STRATEGY

As you think about your strategy, you can write it out or talk about it with friends, family, coworkers, and colleagues. I've found it is helpful to be deliberate with your plan of action, even if it does change as you go along. It probably will change, but talking about it and writing it down will help you stick to your plan. Writing about my giving pledge, for example, held me accountable when I committed to donating money to charity on a regular basis instead of waiting until the end of the year.

You may already have some ideas about new ways to incorporate giving into your everyday life. Maybe you've even started to act on some of those ideas. I will leave you with five final action steps to develop a simple everyday giving strategy.

1. *Think About Why You Want to Give More*

    I will ask you one more time: Why did you pick up this book? What is motivating you to read about giving? Is there a certain cause that keeps you up at night? Whom do you feel most compelled to help? If you had an unlimited amount of money at your disposal, how would you use it to change the world? Spelling out exactly what motivates you and what impact you'd like to have are important first steps in creating your everyday giving strategy.

2. *Choose at Least One Giving Model You Will Commit to Taking Action On*

    Was there a giving model or story that resonated with you more than the others? Go back and review those chapters, stories, and action steps that spoke to you the most. You might take some time and visit some of the websites of the people and companies mentioned. You can start as small or as big as you'd like. The key is to choose at least one giving model to focus on.

3. *Look Through the Resources and Find Your Own*

    Don't try to reinvent the wheel with your giving. There is certainly room for creativity, as we've seen in the stories that illustrate each giving model, but you don't need to start from scratch. There are many resources available in this book and beyond. Read articles about finding your passion. Do research on the causes and charities you'd like to support. Look for stories about people performing good deeds. Find new places and products you will feel good about visiting and purchasing. Research different business designations. Search for potential like-minded partners in your quest to give. The more research you do, the easier your strategy will be to implement.

4. *Define Your Goals for Simple Giving*

Now that you have a better idea of why you are giving, how you are giving, and what impact you'd like to make, write down a few goals. Again, these can be as big or as small as you'd like. Your goals could be as simple as performing one act of kindness per month and making an effort to shop at the local farmers' market every week. Your goal could be to raise funds for a local nonprofit through proceeds from a product you sell or to learn more about philanthropy by joining a giving circle. Setting goals can help you measure the effectiveness of your giving strategy. You want to make them achievable, but not so easy that you aren't motivated to give more.

5. *Go out and Be a Simple Giver!*

Enough reading, writing, talking, and researching. It's time to go out and give! There are so many ways to give every day. Start taking those action steps to give more. Get the idea out of your head that you need lots of money and time to give back in a meaningful way. Grab some friends and bring them along for the ride. Inspire others to join you. Take a few risks, if you can. You'll be amazed at what you can accomplish when you are committed to making giving a part of everyday life.

BECOME A SIMPLE GIVER: RESOURCES

- Simple Giving Lab (www.simplegivinglab.com): The mission of Simple Giving Lab, the website that I created when I was writing this book, is simple: to inspire others to give back every single day. Take a look at the inspiring stories that are shared on the blog or submit your own inspiration for simple giving (www.simplegivinglab.com/submit). You can also stay connected to Simple Giving by joining our e-mail list.

- Nonprofits I Support (www.anotherjennifer.com/giving-back /nonprofits-i-support): I created this list to help keep track of the nonprofits I was working with, writing about, and supporting financially. The neat thing is that you can use my list to create your own. Pick some of mine and add other nonprofits to your list. It's easy, and you can keep track of the causes you are supporting or would like to support.

- "5 Ways to Find and Navigate Your Passion When You're Totally Bored of the Usual Routine" (www.huffingtonpost .com/rakel-sosa/5-ways-to-find-and-navigate-your -passion_b_6497788.html): An article by Rakel Sosa that includes strategies she has used to "navigate passion so you can smoothly get into it and turn your life on."

- *The Paradox of Generosity: Giving We Receive, Grasping We Lose*: A book by Christian Smith and Hilary Davidson. "Offering a wide range of vividly illustrative case studies, this volume will be a crucial resource for anyone seeking to understand the true impact and meaning of generosity."

NOTES

Chapter 1: Acting on the Pull to Give

1. http://anotherjennifer.com/the-meaning-of-philanthropy/
2. http://matthewsm1th.com/2011/11/23/the-difference-between-charity-and-philanthropy/
3. http://money.cnn.com/2010/07/09/news/international/haiti_donation/
4. http://anotherjennifer.com/philanthropy-friday-giving-smiles-and-support/
5. http://www.talkaboutgiving.org/
6. http://anotherjennifer.com/philanthropy-friday-generosity-as-a-business-model/
7. http://www.npr.org/sections/health-shots/2012/12/27/168128084/random-acts-of-kindness-can-make-kids-more-popular

Chapter 2: The Psychology of Giving

1. http://www.ted.com/talks/martin_seligman_on_the_state_of_psychology
2. http://www.dailygood.org/story/603/how-to-make-giving-feel-good-elizabeth-w-dunn-michael-i-norton/

   http://www.psychologicalscience.org/index.php/publications/observer/2013/may-june-13/the-compassionate-mind.html

3. http://greatergood.berkeley.edu/article/item/how_to_make_giving_feel_good
4. http://greatergood.berkeley.edu/article/item/the_top_10_insights_from_the_science_of_a_meaningful_life_in_2013
5. http://www.psychologicalscience.org/index.php/publications/observer/2013/may-june-13/the-compassionate-mind.html
6. http://greatergood.berkeley.edu/article/item/the_top_10_insights_from_the_science_of_a_meaningful_life_in_2013
7. http://www.dailygood.org/story/579/kindness-emotions-david-disalvo/
8. http://anotherjennifer.com/why-giving-feels-good-part-one/
9. http://www.conecomm.com/2013-social-impact
10. http://www.dailygood.org/story/603/how-to-make-giving-feel-good-elizabeth-w-dunn-michael-i-norton/
11. http://anotherjennifer.com/philanthropy-friday-smile-and-change-your-world/

Chapter 3: Giving Model 1: Everyday Acts of Kindness

1. http://www.psychologicalscience.org/index.php/publications/observer/2013/may-june-13/the-compassionate-mind.html

2. http://anotherjennifer.com
   /philanthropy-friday-100-days-400
   -acts-of-kindness/
3. http://anotherjennifer.com
   /philanthropy-friday-making-an
   -impact-one-mitzvah-at-a-time/

Chapter 4: Giving Model 2:
A New Approach to Traditional
Philanthropy

1. http://magazine.good.is/articles
   /six-lessons-learned-while-pledging-to
   -donate-every-month
2. http://www.theguardian.com
   /sustainable-business/2014/dec/08
   /new-age-of-philanthropy
   -philanthropreneurship
3. http://philanthropy.com/article
   /As-Wealthy-Give-Smaller-Share
   /152481
4. https://medium.com/@anotherjenb
   /reframing-philanthropy
   -63209927e0bf
5. http://anotherjennifer.com
   /everydayhero/

Chapter 5: Giving Model 3:
Shopping with a Conscience

1. http://www.conecomm.com
   /2013-social-impact
2. http://www.conecomm.com
   /2013-global-csr-study-report
3. http://anotherjennifer.com
   /philanthropy-friday-scoring-climate
   -leadership/

Chapter 6: Giving Model 4:
Taking Action on Your Passion

1. Original Philanthropy Friday post:
   http://anotherjennifer.com
   /philanthropy-friday-building
   -education-in-tanzania/

2. Original Philanthropy Friday post:
   http://anotherjennifer.com
   /philanthropy-friday-sensing-a-need/
3. Original Philanthropy Friday post:
   http://anotherjennifer.com
   /philanthropy-friday-molly-bears/

Chapter 7: Giving Model 5:
Giving as a Business Model

1. http://www.conecomm.com
   /2013-social-impact
2. http://anotherjennifer.com
   /philanthropy-friday-enjoy-one
   -share-one/
3. http://anotherjennifer.com
   /philanthropy-friday-relax
   -and-do-good/

Chapter 8: Giving Model 6:
Giving It Forward

1. http://www.mcclatchydc.com/2009
   /05/19/68455/tips-for-raising
   -generous-children.html
2. http://www.talkaboutgiving.org
   /recent-studies-indicate-altruism-in
   -babies-toddlers/
3. http://anotherjennifer.com
   /harnessing-the-power-of-social
   -good-moms/
4. http://www.pplkind.com/culture
   /looking-at-the-world-through-a
   -different-view-finder/

Chapter 9: Become a Simple Giver

1. http://www.newrepublic.com/article
   /119477/science-generosity-why
   -giving-makes-you-happy/
2. http://www.one.org/us/2015/03/26
   /using-the-power-of-community-for
   -advocacy-on-worldwaterday/

Drawing on the wisdom of great thinkers past and present, as well as cutting-edge scientific research, Jenny Santi makes an eloquent and passionate case that oftentimes the answers to the problems that haunt us, and the key to the happiness that eludes us, lie in helping those around us.

978-0-39917-549-7 • $25.95

"When all is said and done, it all comes down to kindness. This book says it all and should become a classic. Highly and enthusiastically recommended to all."

—RICHARD CARLSON, author of *Don't Sweat the Small Stuff*

978-1-58542-588-4 • $13.95

If you enjoyed this book, visit

www.tarcherbooks.com

and sign up for Tarcher's e-newsletter to receive
special offers, giveaway promotions, and
information on hot upcoming releases.

TARCHER
PENGUIN

Great Lives Begin with Great Ideas

Connect with the Tarcher Community

. . .

Stay in touch with favorite authors!
Enter weekly contests!
Read exclusive excerpts!
Voice your opinions!

Follow us

 Tarcher Books

 @TarcherBooks

If you would like to place a bulk order
of this book, call 1-800-847-5515.